REDEEMING THE BEREAVED:

A SPIRITUAL MODEL FOR HEALING OUR WOUNDEDNESS

By
James A. Houck, Jr., Ph.D.

PRESS

INTRODUCTION

There's a scar on my left thumb. I was seventeen at the time, working on a mock-roofing project designed to teach us students how to shingle a roof properly. My task was to cut smaller sections of shingles so they would fit at the end of each row. It was about an hour before quitting time, and of course, as with most avoidable accidents, I was in a hurry to finish a job. With my straight-edge in one hand and my utility knife in the other, I began to score the section that needed to be cut. On the fourth pass, the knife seemed to jump across the straight-edge and across my left thumb. Thereafter, I finished the day in the emergency room, getting seven stitches for my haste.

Reflecting on that experience has taught me a lot about the natural progression of recovering from painful experiences. When I was cut, I experienced the excruciating pain of a fresh wound. In the days that followed, whenever I accidentally bumped my thumb, the pain and blood reminded me that although the wound was stitched, healing was still a long way off. Now, decades later, I am still reminded of that day, not because of the pain, but because of the scar.

All of us have scars from previous wounds. Some are more obvious than others, such as a wound from surgery or an accident. Other scars, however, are not so obvious. These scars, resulting from certain emotional and spiritual wounds, are kept hidden deep within our hearts and souls. Very rarely do we permit others to touch these wounds perhaps because we never were healed from them. Some wounds are still fresh, even from five, 10, 15 or more years ago. In these incidences, a scar has never formed, because we never have allowed the healing process to take place. We are constantly poking at the wound, scratching open the scab, and reliving the painful memories all over again. And despite our mothers' warnings that it "*will never heal unless you stop picking at it,*" we still apply the temporary band-aids of prescription or illegal drugs and alcohol, repression, denial, or some other sedating relief.

The same process could be said regarding finding healing from the emotional wounds of loss and grief. However, a common misunderstanding is that once we have assimilated our losses, we will go back to where we were before the loss: our original emotional and spiritual state. This "return to the way things were" rarely happens. Instead, we are constantly shaped and changed by our losses. Once we have experienced a loss, our outlook on life is forever altered by the grief we sustain. The reason for this is because our assumptions about life, and the world in which we live, have now been challenged. We have become accustomed to the routines which define our daily existence. Furthermore, we will never see ourselves, others and/or the world the same as we once did, because we are pulled into the task of trying to make sense out of new circumstances in light of the old.

Yet, instead of assimilating our losses into our everyday lives, many people resist this healing by continuing to live in a prison of bitterness reinforced by the familiar patterns of abuse, low self-esteem, feelings of unworthiness, contempt, jealousy, strife, etc. Instead of looking for the potential of being made better by our losses, we allow bitterness to harden our hearts and keep others out, all the while cementing the anguish inside. The challenge, then, is for us discover the courage to redefine ourselves in light of our pain and grief. Still, we are compelled to ask this question: Is this assimilation process something we are able to do on our own, or do we need help from others?

Today, when I look at my thumb I see more than just a scar; more than just a reminder of a painful time in my past. I also see a thumbprint, something we all have in common, with no two are alike. It's what identifies us as unique, among other characteristics. These prints are one of the most distinguishable parts of our bodies. Hospitals record them as a means of identifying newborns and their mothers. Certain jobs require applicants to get finger-printed prior to employment. Even people who have been arrested have their prints taken as a matter of legal record. All in all, our fingerprints can tell a lot about us. So do our scars. They identify what wounds we have suffered as a result of the past: accidents, mistakes, surgeries and unfortunate mishaps of being in the wrong place at the wrong time. The same could be said for our bereavement. We all experience loss and grief throughout our lives, but just as no two thumbprints are alike, so too do no two people grieve in the same manner, or react similarly to parts of the loss experience.

In the past, not much has been said regarding the psycho spiritual nature of redemption as it relates to assimilating losses into our lives. Most of what has been written has come from a strict theological viewpoint, i.e., defining redemption exclusively as the removal of sin, thus restoring a person to his/her previous stature in the community of faith. In other words, Christ not only forgave the sin in people's lives, but also healed the psychological and emotional wounds that resulted from social stigma and prejudice. Furthermore, people who were once disenfranchised because of specific losses now celebrated the restoration of their dignity and worth in themselves, the community, and ultimately the Kingdom of Heaven. Estadt (1991) states: "*Jesus came, not to change the human condition but to embrace it. He came, not to take away human suffering but to give it meaning in terms of the resurrection.*" When placed within the context of how Christ interacted with others, redemption takes on a deeper significance and responsibility for people of faith to either become part of the healing or hindering process. When communities are part of the healing process of loss and grief, they empower the bereft to then go of their pain and be redeemed from their losses.

In our search for meaning following loss, we often overlook the relationship between the intrapsychic (how we view ourselves) and interpersonal (how we view others) components of bereavement. As communal people of faith, we are constantly in relationship with ourselves, others, and God. The three associations can never be separated. How we see ourselves, as well as what we tell ourselves about ourselves, is just as important as how we see others and our relationship with God.

Therefore, by examining redemption in this manner, it can provide a spiritual model for healing from the wounds of loss and grief. As a result, this book is divided into three sections: *Our Wounds* focuses on how loss and grief affect us physically, emotionally, and spiritually. *Our Scars* looks at how loss and grief function as the emotional reminders of the pain we have experienced in our lives. In the final section, *Our Redemption* looks at the biblical theme of redemption as a spiritual model for healing loss and grief, as well as empowering others to understand their emotional scars as a source of empathy and strength to others.

Praise be to the God and Father of our Lord Jesus Christ, the Father of all compassion and the God of all comfort, who comforts us in all our troubles, so that we can comfort those in any trouble with the comfort we have received from God. 2 Corinthians 1:3-4 (NIV)

OUR WOUNDS

Painful Experiences

There's a natural progression to healing that takes place in our bodies whenever we are wounded. Take, for example, the scar on my left thumb. When I initially cut my thumb, there was immediate pain and blood. Medical experts tell us that pain is not necessarily a bad thing; it's our body's way of telling us there's something wrong. The pain can be excruciating at times, which is our body's way of telling us something is *really* wrong. For example, if we place our hand on a hot stove, pain signals the brain telling us to remove our hand, now! All of this is done in a split second; otherwise, we would risk further serious injury. At any rate, when we are cut, we bleed. Again, it's our body's way not only of telling us something's wrong, but also of helping to cleanse the wound from dirt. Of course, we need to stop the bleeding at some point, often the sooner the better. However, some people, who have lost some or all of the feeling in a part of the body, must exercise extra caution as they could accidentally cut themselves and not be aware of it.

Once the bleeding has stopped a scab begins to form over the next couple of days. At this point, there's a "healing from the inside out" occurring. If the cut is deep enough, stitches are needed to close the wound, and antibiotics are taken to ward off infection. Once the wound has been completely healed, the scab dries up and falls off naturally. Depending of the depth and size of the wound, a scar may remain as a reminder of the pain we experienced. Of course, the deeper the wound, the more intense the pain will be, and the longer this healing process will take.

During this process, many people are able to find some relief from the pain through prescribed medications or other medical interventions. Again, this is a good thing for overall we are a people who cannot tolerate physical pain. If you have any doubt about this, just go to your medicine cabinet and take a quick inventory of everything located there designed to eliminate or dull your pain: aspirin, antacid tablets, cold sore gel, lip-balm, arthritis medication, etc. These are all items we can buy over the counter. Some people will anesthetize themselves from the pain through illegal drugs, alcohol, or other means of escaping what is unbearable to them.

Many times an initial means of anesthetizing can lead to addictions. What begins as an easy way to eliminate pain quickly evolves into a habitual abuse or dependence on alcohol, drugs, or other substances. One of the most accurate descriptions I've discovered regarding understanding the reason why half the people in rehab relapse from an addiction within the first three months of starting treatment, and 75% by the first year, comes from Ernie Larsen (1984) who states that overcoming addictions is a two-stage process: One, is the initial stage or withdrawal, during which the substance or toxin has to be physically removed from the body. Larsen relates this stage to a sort of "boot-camp," in that just as a soldier completes his/her initial military training, so too does an addicted person begin the initial steps of becoming clean and sober. A common misunderstanding made by those who struggle with addictions is that they believe that a "three-day detox" is all that is necessary in order to kick the physical desire for the substance. Wrong. Ironically, this initial, but extremely important step, involves only 10% of the work needed to remain clean and sober. The rest of the work (90%) is what Larsen refers to as Stage II. I like to call it "the rest of your life." To overcome any type of addictive behavior, a person must address the psychological and spiritual issues that underlie dependence. While it's one thing for a user/abuser to rid him/herself of ingesting physically damaging substances, it's quite another thing to recognize and overcome the "triggers" that entice him/her to use. These triggers can include anything from how he/she handles (or not) stressful experiences, continues to reinforce distorted perceptions, to unhealthy habits in one's daily routine. Just ask dieticians who work with people trying to lose weight and they will tell you that in addition to portion control and exercise, the key to cutting pounds is the dieters' changing attitudes and perceptions about why they eat what they do. Whether or not we want to admit it, in the matter of sustaining healthy behaviors, we are often our own worst enemy. Instead of dealing with the root of the problem, some people may engage in either minimizing their personal problems (*It's not that bad after all*) to adopting a fatalistic attitude (*That's just the way things are. There's nothing I can do about*).

So what does all this have to do with our woundedness, emotional or otherwise? Quite simply, everything. Just as physical pain can be unbearable at times, so too can emotional pain be unbearable. Emotional distress often inflicts the wounds we cannot see in each other, but they do affect the ways we see ourselves, others and God. For example, some people who suffer from loneliness may fail to see how they push others away with their cutting remarks when they fear others are getting too close. In other words, they may hold people at a distance because it's too painful when people brush-up against wounds received from years of emotional or verbal abuse.

Years ago I counseled a 40-year old woman who suffered with depression. "Lisa" lamented over one failed relationship after another, often blaming her failures on others.

She had a history of being emotionally abused and rejected by other women in her life, often being made to feel that she did not measure up to unattainable expectations. She had attempted suicide twice in her life and endured two marriages than ended in divorce. Only after intensive work did Lisa recognize a pattern in her life of sabotaging relationships when her physical and emotional intimacy reached a certain depth. It became clear to her that whenever someone started to get too close to her vulnerable self, she panicked and started to push them away by honing in on their character flaws. Interestingly, her behavior of pushing people away was always preceded by her receiving compliments either on her physical appearance, or her excellence at work. Words that were meant to attract and foster friendship and intimacy, Lisa perceived as phony and threatening. The result: before others could hurt her with what she anticipated as more broken promises and unrealistic expectations, she hurt them by being distant, cold, and isolated. By doing so, she was able to justify to herself that these people, who actually cared for her deeply, only wanted to control her. In her mind, it worked. People would begin to separate themselves and eventually avoid her altogether, thus reinforcing her perception that nobody truly cared about her.

This disappointment in life is quite common especially when we look to others for approval, acceptance or define our worth according to their standards. In his work entitled *The Return of the Prodigal Son,* Nouwen (1992) also struggled with measuring up to the expectations of others as he writes,

As long as I keep running about asking: "Do you love me? Do you really love me?" I give all the power to the voices of the world and put myself in bondage because the world is filled with "ifs." The world says: "Yes, I love you if you are good-looking, intelligent, and wealthy. I love you if you have a good education, a good job, and good connections. I love you if you produce much, sell much and buy much." There are endless "ifs" hidden in the world's love. These "ifs" enslave me, since it is impossible to respond adequately to all of them. The world's love is and always will be conditional. As long as I keep looking for my true self in the world of conditional love, I will remain "hooked" to the world—trying, failing and trying again. It is a world that fosters addictions because what it offers cannot satisfy the deepest craving of my heart (page 42).

What helped start to break her vicious cycle of sabotaging relationships was an exercise we did together over several weeks: a little exercise in comparison. First, I asked Lisa to make two columns on a sheet of paper. In column one, she listed all the ways people might give compliments, i.e. how they saw her. In the other column, she described how she felt when she received that compliment, and how she truly wanted to be seen. While this endeavor was not an easy process of healing, I knew we were making significant progress one day when she realized that even if she did not initially believe compliments, she could at least say "thank you." She also elevated her self-esteem by focusing on what gives her joy in life. Despite these insights, with Lisa's emotional wounds going so very deep, it took several years of work to help her not only heal from her past, but also to redefine herself as a woman of competency, value and worth.

I believe with our age of enlightenment logic, we have become a people constantly obsessed with discovering a "first-cause" to our problems. Like dominos cascading one on top of another, we want to stop the perpetual motion of maladaptive behavior and attitudes that cause us pain. Our reasoning suggests that if only we can go back and find the first time we were humiliated or when a confidence was betrayed or even when we lost the innocence of childhood, then we can undo years of suffering and misery. For some people this task is easier than others. Most of the time these earliest memories lie buried deep inside, protected with layers of self-created cement.

As a boy I loved to explore the woods near our home. I would imagine being on some hunt to find lost remains of an ancient civilization, or hacking my way through some deep underbrush of the Serengeti. To my mother's indignation (and often indigestion), I would slosh around in the creek, scale trees with the skill of a monkey, and even return home with the remains of something that would have been better left for the vultures. On occasion, curiosity would get the better of me and I would kick over rocks, just to see what was underneath. Sometimes, I would find nothing. Other times, all sorts of squirmy, slimy insects and amphibious-looking creatures scrambled for cover as the result of having their homes disturbed.

As a therapist and pastor, I am very careful which "rocks" I turn over in a person's life. For some therapists, the anticipation of uncovering what lies beneath may be exhilarating, but for clients, the discovery may be unnerving to say the least. When we start to break up the concrete layers, we may discover all sorts of infestation lurking in the cold, damp darkness. Although what lies beneath may be heinous, repulsive and nauseating from our perspective, for the suffering person safety often lies in keeping the pain in the dark. In his book, *The Gift of Therapy: An Open Letter to a New Generation of Therapists and Their Patients (P.S.),* Irvin Yalom (2009) states that therapy can be as simple as removing the obstacles of faulty assumptions, maladaptive behavior, etc., that hinder a person's growth. Once these obstacles are uncovered, then the natural progression toward self-actualization can occur freely. I like go one-step further. I tell my counseling students that whenever they begin to target problematic behavior in a person's life, that therapy is more than just removing the obstacles. It's also about replacing those behaviors and patterns with positive, life-giving ways of coping. I prefer to use the metaphor of a house that's built on stilts near water. If you start to remove one or more of the problem stilts without hoisting something else in place to keep it above the water line, the whole house collapses. Moreover, I've discovered that it is much more effective for the client to identify which stilts he/she wants to replace and with what stronger supports, and then he/she can work along-side the therapist to achieve this. Even drawing a diagram of a house, labeling each stilt as a particular strength or growing edge can be helpful for clients who would benefit from the visual reminder.

For example, "Bob," a 37 year-old construction worker, had a history of alcohol abuse. Although he claimed that he had no problem as he "only drank on the weekends," he had begun to arrive late for work on Monday mornings. His company had placed him on probation and sent him to me for counseling. As we talked it became obvious that he was "working for the weekend," and used Saturday and Sunday as a time to relax and unwind. Our strategy was that, instead of letting of all the stress and tension build up over the work-week, we started to identify ways in which he could relax each day. Drawing the diagram of the house on stilts really made an impact on Bob as he easily named what areas of his life supported him and which ones were starting to decay. As our sessions progressed, Bob's enthusiasm grew as he started to use construction terms like insulation, concrete and framing, as metaphors for his life. Over time he started to set aside an hour each day for quiet meditation or reading, and even took up fishing and other "constructive" ways of having fun on his weekends.

When I counsel others who are struggling with their symptoms of depression, anxiety, and/or general negative feelings about life itself, sooner or later the focus turns to loss. More than just the death of a loved-one, there are other losses we experience that result from the changes life demands of us: divorce, transfers, career changes, promotions, marriage, failed relationships, graduations, broken dates, etc. In reflection on the clients who come to me, I often ask myself, "What losses have been the most difficult for them? How old were they when had their first loss? What do they remember about it? How did they feel at the time? What part of themselves did they lose and how much of themselves do they wish to have back again?"

Some people in the remote villages of China have a custom that when a woman is married, she is given a double-sided mirror by her mother. When the groom arrives at her home to take his bride to live with his family, she looks first at her face in the mirror as a reminder of the past. Her image in the glass helps her remember who she is and from where she has come. She is never to forget her family, her heritage. Half way on the journey to her husband's home, she then is told to turn the mirror over, and again look at her face. This time, instead of remembering her heritage, she is to see who she is: her present and future as a wife and mother. While not necessarily from China, many of us often struggle our own double-sided mirrors. We may find it difficult to see ourselves in the present, let alone the future, because we have trouble getting beyond the past. Our wounds have a way of keeping us from turning the mirror over.

Loss, Grief, Mourning and Bereavement

A key component to any type of pain (physical, emotional or spiritual) is loss and grief. Whenever we experience change in our lives we also experience a degree of loss from what once was familiar. The result is a grief reaction on some personal level. Jeffreys (2005) makes this concept even easier to remember: Change = Loss = Grief. Now changes in our lives should not be viewed as necessarily a negative thing. In fact, some changes are for the better: Bar Mitzvahs, confirmations, marriages, a new job, moving closer to family, even having surgery to correct an illness or stave off a spreading disease. All these life experiences and others as well have elements of both sorrowful loss and hopeful expectations in them. While we often think of events like a high-school or college graduation ceremony as marking an ending, it's not. Instead, commencement, as the name implies, also marks a beginning. This beginning can be understood as turning a new page in our lives and new opportunities. Unfortunately, tension comes in with what most people fail to recognize, i.e., in dealing with many life-changing events, we have a deep desire to remain with and enjoy the familiar. Even though we may recall our struggles and heart-breaking moments in high-school or college, at other times we miss those days when our biggest concern was whether or not friends and sweethearts would notice our acne at a dance. In contrast, other experiences, such as graduation, a job promotion or even relocation, may bring anticipated excitement as we look forward to what lies ahead. Still, on the heights of expectancy we cannot overlook the fact that we also need to grieve our loss of what once was.

Certain events in my own life testify to this. For example, before our children were 10 years old, our family had moved four times. I was still in school, completing undergraduate and graduate degrees, and each change in school meant a change in location as well. As the children became older, my wife and I grew more and more concerned about how these moves would affect them in forming friendships. We wondered if they would grow up some day to resent those initial transitions, blaming us for their inability to maintain close relationships. To try to make these moves easier on our children, we decided to help them adjust to their new neighborhoods and schools by focusing on making new friends. We encouraged them to be enthusiastic and look forward to meeting new boys and girls their own age, getting involved in sports activities, and even being invited to birthday parties. At the same time, we were aware of their need to stay in contact with the friends they left behind. About once a month they were allowed to call, send pictures and write to their friends in other cities. My wife and I also took a page out of our own parenting book, following similar practices ourselves, and discovered our transitions became much smoother for us too. We had created our own Chinese double-mirror tradition.

Our many departures and arrivals remind me of some of the confusion that surrounds many of the loss-grief terms. For one, many people, writers included, confuse grief with mourning. This is understandable given the way society interchanges the terms, often adding to the ambiguity of thanatology, or *the study of death*. While the words are closely related, each one has a specific context or meaning. For example, *bereavement*, an umbrella term, has been defined as the state of being deprived of someone by death (Kaplan and Sadock, 2002). Corr (1998) broadens this definition by stating that a bereaved person is one who has been robbed, plundered, or stripped of something or someone of value. This latter definition certainly captures the essence of loss.

As a society, we do not do well with bereavement. In our losses, we may believe that what happens to us is so exclusive, we forget about the other side of the thumb; the fact is, however, that change, loss and death are universal. They are events we all face because we exist. As universal as the events, we can never minimize another's loss; it is still unique to them. There's an ancient story about a bereaved mother who brought her dead child to a holy man to be healed. She begged the master to have pity on her and return her child to life. The master agreed to do so, but only if she would first bring him a mustard seed from a house in her village where death had not been. Initially, the woman was excited because this request seemed so simple. She thought, *"Surely, there must be at least one house where death had not visited!"* Finally, she arrived at the first house and asked if they had any mustard seeds for her. She was delighted when she heard they had plenty to give. However, when she told them that the seed had to come from a household where death had not visited, they told her that they buried their father the year before. Disappointed, yet still hopeful, the woman moved to a second house and asked if they could give her a mustard seed. Again, the family had plenty of seeds to give her, but when she heard that they too buried a loved-one, she could not accept the seed. On and on, the woman went from house to house searching for a family who had been spared from death, but to her dismay, she did not find one. Eventually, she came to understand the wisdom of the master; that death comes to all. Silently, she returned to claim her child's body and returned home to bury him in peace.

Joyce Rupp (2009) in *Praying Our Goodbyes: A Spiritual Companion Through Life's Losses and Sorrows*, notes that although we do it often, we are not very good at saying goodbye. She says that we typically say goodbye anywhere from 20-30 times a day. These goodbyes can include saying goodbye to loved-ones as they go off to school or work, saying goodbye to people we meet at the grocery store, even saying goodbye to another whom we have been talking to on the phone. These goodbyes do not seem to trouble us because we tell ourselves that we will see these people again, or we can always pick up the phone and hear their voice one more time. Yet, what about the goodbyes that do trouble us, such as our farewells to loved-ones upon their death? These good-byes may trouble us deeply, because we may not be ready to come to the closure that the word means; we want more time, and we want to be in charge of when and where we take our leave.

If bereavement is a state of being deprived of something or someone, then grief is an emotional reaction when we are deprived. Still, mourning (as we'll see in the section on *Our Scars*) is best understood as the longer-term process of adapting to our losses, the stage in which the majority of grief work is done. This grief reaction occurs on different levels during all types of changes and loss. Supporting this collective idea, Archer (1999) defines grief as a natural human reaction, a universal feature of human existence, irrespective of culture.

Although we grieve many losses in this world, Rando (1993), an expert in the field of grief work, notes that the death of a loved-one is often the most intense and dramatic because it involves the total loss of a relationship. If you ever want to see this emotional reaction to loss in action, just try and take a toy away from a two-year old and you'll see how grief is manifested in adults. Two-year olds who are still dealing with why their favorite toy was taken away, just want it back. . .now! *"It's mine! Mine! Mine! Gimmie it back!"* Of course, all of this verbal protest is accompanied with loud wails, screams, and other expressions of the temper tantrum. Now I ask you, are we adults any different from two-year olds? Before you answer, consider this: when are we ever ready to relinquish our hold on our favorite toy or loved-one? Never. And, what is our typical initial reaction when they are taken from us? If we answer honestly, we would admit that for the most part we are shocked that this kind of anxiety over separation would even occur. We protest, we cry, we wail, and we might even go so far as to throw a fit! But if we are adults, who supposedly have more wisdom resulting from our lived-experiences, why then do we, on occasion, still have these strong reactions? Quite simple. First of all, a little of a two-year old still remains in each us. Second, we grieve the loss of things and relationships because we emotionally attach.

John Bowlby's (1969) Attachment Theory is still widely accepted today as the foundational understanding of how and why we bond. In a nutshell, Attachment Theory affirms that all human beings have the tendency to seek the closeness of another person, to feel secure when that person is present, and to feel anxious when that person is absent, separated. Yet, we are not the only ones who express these needs. Attachment Theory actually originated with the observation and experiments with animals.

Dr. Harry F. Harlow (1959) believed that the first love of an infant is for his/her mother. In a series of experiments involving monkeys, Harlow demonstrated that an infant's attachment is not a merely a reaction to such internal drives as hunger. In these experiments, young monkeys were separated from their mothers shortly after birth. To serve as "surrogates," two dolls were used. The first doll had a body constructed of wire mesh; the second doll, a body of soft cloth and foam. Both dolls could provide food to the infants through milk bottles attached to their chests. The experiment was designed to see if the infant monkeys would cling to the doll providing the soft contact of cloth or to the doll solely providing the source of food. The result was that the monkeys cuddled with the soft-clothed doll more, whether or not they were nursing. Furthermore, the monkeys also explored more of their environment when the soft-cloth doll was near, indicating to Harlow that this doll provided them with a sense of security. Still, these surrogates could not replace the real thing. The infant monkeys had a better response to their mothers who provided more reciprocal interaction. While Harlow's result were dramatic, profound and a landmark, many people questioned whether the idea that the attachment of human children to their caregivers goes far beyond a desire for fulfilling biological needs?

While being part of the research team at the Tavistock Clinic, researcher Mary Ainsworth (1978) and Connell & Goldsmith (1982) investigated what effects a mother's separation would have on her child's development. She and her colleagues developed the "strange situation" procedure used to assess infant attachment style. The procedure consisted of the following eight steps:

- Parent and infant are introduced to the experimental room.
- Parent and infant are alone. Parent does not participate while infant explores.
- Stranger enters, converses with parent, then approaches infant. Parent leaves inconspicuously.
- First separation episode: Stranger's behavior is geared to that of infant.
- First reunion episode: Parent greets and comforts infant, then leaves again.
- Second separation episode: Infant is alone.
- Continuation of second separation episode: Stranger enters and gears behavior to that of infant.
- Second reunion episode: Parent enters, greets infant, and picks up infant; stranger leaves inconspicuously.

Ainsworth believed that, by observing the infant's behavior upon the mother's return, the experimenter could classify into one of three attachment categories: In the first category, infants described as *securely attached* actively sought out contact with their mothers. They may or may not protest when she leaves the room, but when she returns they approach her and maintain contact. Infants appearing distressed demonstrated a desire to be comforted by their mothers rather than by a stranger, indicating a clear preference for his/her mother. In the second category, an infant who is classified as *avoidant*, demonstrates a clear avoidance of any contact with the mother. For example, the infant may turn away from her or even refusing to make eye contact with her. Ironically, avoidant babies may seem to prefer the stranger, and even appear to be comforted by the stranger when they are distressed. Lastly, a *resistant* infant may initially seek contact with his/her mother upon her return, but then push her away or even turn away from her. Although the infant may demonstrate no particular preference for the stranger, he/she appears angry toward both the mother and the stranger.

Building upon this work, Main and Solomon (1990) described a fourth pattern of attachment behavior: a *disorganized or disoriented behavior.* Under this classification, an infant may appear to have no clear strategy for responding to his/her mother. At times the infant would avoid or resist her approaches to him/her. The infant may also seem confused or frightened by the mother, or freeze when she approaches him/her. All in all, Ainsworth noted that a child's initial response to being separated from his/her mother only intensifies the attachment. The child not only protests the separation, but also attempts to regain contact with the mother by all means.

Interestingly, forming attachments is considered normal behavior that continues throughout our lives, and also impacts the way people experience grief. Whether as a child or adult, forming attachments with significant others comes out of a need for safety, security, and ultimately survival. In terms of grief, Attachment Theory provides a model not only to conceptualize the tendency in human beings to make strong affective bonds with others, but also to understand the strong emotional reaction that occurs when those bonds are broken. For example, any change in the attachment, e.g. separation, creates a loss (real or perceived), in turn produces grief. The more secure emotional attachment a person has to a deceased loved one and the greater his/her ability to adapt to changes in his/her social function following the death, the more effectively a person can relinquish the former bond and form new attachments. Although this process may be described as a normal progression of grief and mourning, it is easier said than done. In fact, half the battle is recognizing how loss and grief can affect us.

Wounds With Many Layers

A common misconception about grief is that it is one-dimensional, i.e., experienced solely as emotional turmoil. Instead, grief is a multi-faceted experience, causing a disruption in a person's physical, emotional, spiritual, social, and philosophical well-being. Worden (2008) proposes that the grief reaction can be categorized into four areas: (1) feelings, (2) physical sensations, (3) cognitions, and (4) behaviors.

Feelings

Sadness

Sorrow accompanied with or without tears;

Anger

Frustration because either nothing else could have been
done to prevent the death, or something could
have been done but was not;

Guilt and Self-Reproach

Manifested around something that happened or neglected at
the time of death;

Anxiety

Fears over survivors not being able to take care of
themselves, and a heightened sense of
personal death awareness;

Loneliness

Expressed by survivors who experienced a close, day-to-
day relationship with the deceased;

Fatigue

Apathy or listlessness;

Helplessness
Sense of being vulnerable and unable to
care for self or others;

Shock
Feeling dazed at the finality of death;

Yearning
Yearning for someone who is unattainable;

Emancipation
Sense of being freed from a difficult environment or
situation, of which the deceased controlled;

Relief
Sense of an emotional burden being lifted, especially if the
loved one suffered a lengthy or painful illness;

Numbness
Typically experienced immediately following
the news of the loved one's death.

Physical Sensations
Hollowness in the stomach
Tightness in the chest
Tightness in the throat
Over-sensitivity to noise

Sense of depersonalization

Breathlessness, feeling short of breath

Weakness in the muscles

Lack of energy

Dry mouth

Cognitions

Disbelief

"There must be some mistake, I can't believe this is happening;"

Confusion

Difficulty in concentrating or survivors forgetting things;

Preoccupation

Obsessive thoughts about the deceased;

Sense of Presence

Survivor may think the deceased is, somehow, still in the current area of time and space;

Hallucinations

Visual and/or auditory illusory experiences, typically occurring within a few weeks of the loss.

Behaviors

Sleep Disturbances
Difficulty going to sleep or staying asleep;

Appetite Disturbances
Can be manifested in overeating or under-eating;

Absentminded Behavior
Forgetfulness in one's daily routine that may cause harm or inconvenience;

Social Withdrawal
Detaching oneself from other people and/or places;

Dreams of the Deceased
May include normal dreams or nightmares;

Avoiding Reminders of the Deceased
Survivors may avoid places or things that trigger painful feelings of grief;

Searching and Calling Out
Calling out the name of the deceased in an attempt to have them answer to return;

Sighing
Similar to the sensation of breathlessness.

Restless Over-Activity
Sense of having the need to remain busy;

Crying
Release of emotional stress;

Visiting Places or Carrying Objects
May arise out a fear of losing a "connection"
with the deceased;

Treasuring Objects That Belonged to the Deceased
Maintain a close connection with the deceased.

In spite of the complexity of how grief is manifested, these experiences are considered as normal reactions, which usually diminish in intensity over time (Kaplan and Sadock, 2002). Still, when I counsel a person who has recently lost a loved-one, the first question I ask after listening to their story is, *"How long has it been since your last complete physical?"* Most of the time people report that it has been three to five years since their last exam. What they are not aware of is just how much life changes after loss; especially the death of a loved-one creates stressful situations for us. If left unchecked, our bodies have a way of carrying those wounds around until they threaten our health significantly.

Eric Lindemann's (1944) initial work with acute grief reactions was ground-breaking in terms of how unresolved grief is a factor in many psychosomatic illnesses. In a paper presented to the Massachusetts Psychiatric Society in February 1942, Lindemann noted that the psychiatric treatment for ulcerative colitis centered on the problem of helping grieving patients achieve the readjustment necessitated by the loss of a loved one. Nine months later in November 1942, Lindemann, observing the grief reactions of those who lost loved ones in the Coconut Grove Nightclub fire, saw similar psychosomatic characteristics resulting from mourning a beloved person who died in the fire. These observations led Lindermann (1986) to formulate three stages of grief work: (1) emancipation from the bondage to the deceased, (2) readjustment to the environment in which the deceased is missing, and (3) the formation of new relationships.

In 1967 psychologist Thomas Holmes and Navy scientist Richard Rahe developed a scale that measured how susceptible people were to developing illness based on a rating of stressful events they were experiencing over a two-year period. The Holmes and Rahe Social Readjustment Scale (below) allows people to determine the total amount of stress accumulated within a year by adding up stress values, known as Life Change Units (LCU). Acquiring 200 or more Life Change Units increases the risk of mental health imbalance, including anxiety and depression. Persons with a low stress tolerance may find themselves overstressed with a score of 150. According to Holmes and Rahe a score of 150 or less indicates a 37% chance of becoming seriously ill. If a person scores between 150 to 300 LCU's, their chances increase to 51%. Over 300 and there's an 80% chance of serious illness.

Life Event	Life Changing Units
Death of spouse	100
Divorce	73
Separation from living partner	65
Jail term or probation	63
Death of close family member other than spouse	63
Serious personal injury or illness	53
Marriage or establishing a life partnership	50
Fired at work	47
Marital or relationship reconciliation	45
Retirement	45
Change in health of immediate family member	44
Work more than 40 hours per week	40
Pregnancy or causing pregnancy	40
Sex difficulties	39
Gain of new family member	39
Business or work role change	39
Change in financial state	38
Death of a close friend (not a family member)	37
Change in number of arguments with spouse or life partner	35
Mortgage or loan for a major purchase or purpose	31
Foreclosure of mortgage or loan	30

Change in responsibilities at work or at home	29
Trouble with in-laws or with children	29
Outstanding personal achievement	28
Spouse begins or stops work	26
Begin or end school	26
Change in living conditions (long-term visitors, remodeling)	25
Change in personal habits (diet, exercise, smoking)	24
Trouble with boss	23
Change in work hours or conditions	20
Moving to new residence	20
Change in schools	20
Change in religious activities	19
Change in social activities (more or less than before)	18
Minor financial loan	17
Change in frequency of family get-togethers	15
Vacation	13
Presently in winter holiday season	13
Minor violation of the law	11

TOTAL SCORE: _____

Although the Holmes and Rahe Stress Scale is somewhat dated, it is still widely used to demonstrate how stress correlates with illness. It is a quick tool everyone can use to assess how positive and negative changes in our lives affect us physically and emotionally.

Anticipatory Grief: Anticipating the wounds

> *When the doctor told me I had cancer, it felt as though my heart dropped down into my stomach. I just sat there stunned, feeling a little dizzy, not knowing what to say. I couldn't say anything because I couldn't believe what he was telling me. Soon, all of his words like "tests, support groups, chemotherapy, life-expectancy, infertility, more tests and remission," all became jumbled together. I could hear his words, but they meant nothing to me at the time. My stomach was in knots. When I got home, I vomited in the toilet. All I could do was to sit down on the bathroom floor, doubled-over with a feeling of being kicked in the stomach. I couldn't move.*

> Lewis, age 54, diagnosed with prostate cancer

Many people react differently to the news of a terminal illness. Lewis' reaction to the news of being diagnosed with cancer may not be typical of everyone, but one thing's for sure: as soon as we are confronted with our own mortality, either by the news of a fatal disease of our own or that of a loved-one, we grieve. Irvin Yalom (1980), a leading author and practitioner of existential psychotherapy, would call this type of reaction "death-anxiety." For example, when we think of anxiety, we might first think of ways to rid ourselves of all moments of feeling anxious. Yet ironically, Yalom has a different approach. He believes that anxiety is not necessarily a bad thing. In fact, what we often mistake for anxiety is actually our own reaction to anxiety. For example, if we are asked to speak in front of a crowd we may feel anxious. Our skin begins to perspire, our hearts beat faster and we may even feel some tightness in our stomach. So what do we do? We look for all kinds of antidotes to feel better: self-talk, medication to calm our nerves, even believing that a shot of whiskey will settle us down. All of these things and other antidotes offer temporary relief, but never get at the root of what may be causing anxiety in the first place. When people sit with their anxiety, embrace it, and listen to its meaning, they soon discover what's really going on; namely, fear. When speaking in public, we may fear looking and sounding ridiculous. We may be fear being humiliated. We may fear that we will forget what we want to say. We may even fear, since all eyes are on us, that we really don't have anything worth saying.

Translating this "fear" to our subject of anticipatory grief, death-anxiety brings us face to face with our own mortality. Being anxious then is quite normal. What needs to be discussed is our fear of death and all that that entails. For instance, we may be afraid of the process of dying and the pain associated with that. We may fear being separated from our loved-ones and not knowing if they can look after themselves. We may fear the unknown of what comes after our last breath.

When my mother was diagnosed with pulmonary fibrosis, the disease too quickly progressed to the point of allowing her only three weeks to live. My nuclear family took turns taking care of her, with me taking the midnight shift from 11pm-7am. Without fail, every morning about 2am, she lie in her bed wide awake and ready to talk. We talked about everything we ever wanted to say to each other. We prayed together and sang hymns some times. One night she looked upset and shared how much she worried about leaving "us kids" alone (although we were all in our 30's and 40's). I told her not to worry, that we would be fine. I also reassured her that when "her time was near," she could peacefully let go. With a solemn look in her eyes, Mom said, *"I don't know how to do that."* I replied, *"Then just let go of our hands and take hold of God's hands, and let God lead you home."* Surprisingly, that's all I needed to say. Her fears subsided and she was then able to rest more comfortably. About a week later, she was able to go home.

The fear of death permeates every part of our society, from movies to art, even to what people talk about in workplace lunchrooms. Yet, most of the dreaded talk reinforces a kind of existential prison in which the subject death is deemed so taboo that we never realize how much we fear living to the fullest. Yalom (1980) puts it another way: *"Death and life are interdependent: though the physicality of death destroys us, the idea of death saves us.*"

Some people may say that Lewis' grief from being diagnosed with cancer was delayed because he reported not feeling anything due to the shock of his own illness. Yet, if we think about it, once we are able to comprehend that death is real and that someday we too shall die (despite how disturbing that may be for us), our world-view changes. It changes from the naïve innocence of immortality, pleasure and being cared for, to a realization that we must confront our own sickness, aging and death. There's an ancient story told of the spiritual journey of an Indian man called Siddhartha during the time of the Buddha that illustrates this point.

Siddhartha was born around 563 B.C., in Kapilavastu, India into the clan of the Shakyas, a warrior tribe inhabiting an area just below the Himalayan foothills. While he was an infant, it was prophesized that Siddhartha would have a tremendous impact on humanity by either becoming a great ruler or a great religious sage. His father the king, eager that Siddhartha should also become king, was determined to shield him from anything disturbing that might result in his taking up the religious life. And so Siddhartha was kept in one or another of their three palaces, and was prevented from experiencing much of what ordinary people might consider quite commonplace. For instance, he was not permitted to see the elderly, the sickly, the dead, or anyone who had dedicated themselves to ascetic spiritual practices. Only beauty and health surrounded Siddhartha. Despite living in the luxury of his palaces, Siddhartha grew increasing restless and curious about the world beyond the palace walls. He finally demanded that he be permitted to see his people and his lands. The king carefully arranged that Siddhartha should still not see the kind of suffering that he feared would lead him to a religious life, and decreed that only young and healthy people should greet the prince.

Yet, what Siddhartha saw one particular day changed his life forever. That day Siddhartha went out riding with his charioteer Chandaka. As he left the palace, he came upon an old man with bent body and legs trembling with the decrepitude of age. Slowly, walking painfully and leaning heavily upon his stick, the old man was struggling down the road. Siddhartha had never before seen the infirmity of the elderly. He pulled his chariot to a halt and asked Chandaka why this man was the way he was? Chandaka replied that the man was old and his body, failing. In an anguished voice, Siddhartha asked if all human beings were destined to grow old as that man and Chandaka replied this was a fact of life. Siddhartha returned to the palace in a troubled state of mind. Shortly after this, the Prince went riding along another road that led southwards out of the city. He hadn't gone far when he saw a man who was desperately ill. The sight shocked him and he stopped to ask Chandaka what the matter was. Chandaka replied that the man was dying and no one could help him. Once again the Prince returned home in a troubled mood. Later, he again left the city and saw a dead body being carried to the cremation ground. Behind the body walked a group of people wailing and crying. Siddhartha asked Chandaka why the people were so sad? Chandaka replied that the man on the litter had died and his family was grieving because they would never see him again. Again, disturbed and anguished by what he had seen, Siddhartha returned home. A short while later the Siddhartha went riding along the road leading northwards. He saw a monk dressed in saffron robes. The monk carried a begging bowl in his hand and he walked along the road with an aura of peace. Siddhartha was struck by the man's calmness and asked Chandaka who the monk was and why he was dressed that way? Chandaka replied that the monk had renounced the world and all material possessions and in doing so had found a measure of serenity. He explained that the monk and others like him were engaged in trying to discover truth. All of these experiences awakened compassion within the heart of Siddhartha. Shortly afterwards, he made the decision to renounce his lavish lifestyle and go on a spiritual pilgrimage in quest of truth in order to find a path (which later became known as Buddhism or the Way of the Buddha) for others to follow that would put an end to their pain.

Adapted from *Siddhartha*, Hermann Hesse (2005)

Within Buddhism, there's a belief that there is nothing fixed and permanent in this world: Everything and everyone is subject to change, or as the Buddha taught, in "a continuous becoming." We refer to this as *impermanence*. If you have ever sat beside a river and watched its flow, you get the idea. The water runs from point to point, around rocks and fallen branches, finding the way of least resistance. At the same time, the river is not one continuous and unified flow. The river of this moment is not going to be the same as the river of the next moment. Hence comes the saying from the ancient philosopher Heraclitus, *"You cannot not step into the same river twice; for other waters are ever flowing on to you."*

This same philosophy can be applied to our lives. None of us remains the same throughout our years. The various stages of our lives, from childhood to adulthood to old age, are not the same at any given time. The child is not the same when he/she grows up and becomes a young adult, nor when he/she grows elderly. From a biological understanding we know that old cells in our bodies die and yield places continuously to the new ones that are forming. While it is true that we live from moment to moment, we tend to forget that each moment leads to the next. Impermanence and change are thus the undeniable truths of our existence. The Apostle Paul echoes this observation from a Christian perspective in 2 Corinthians 4:16-18,

Therefore we do not lose heart. Though outwardly we are wasting away, yet inwardly we are being renewed day by day. For our light and momentary troubles are achieving for us an eternal glory that far outweighs them all. So we fix our eyes not on what is seen, but on what is unseen. For what is seen is temporary, but what is unseen is eternal.

The term Anticipatory (or preparatory) Grief can be somewhat confusing. Whereas our grief reaction normally occurs after the death of a loved-one, sometimes without warning, anticipatory grief is our reaction when we see loss or death coming in the near future. In the case of death, I am convinced that people who are in the final stages of a terminal illness are quite aware of what is taking place. They notice physical changes in themselves, e.g., loss of energy, appetite, weight and muscle mass, etc. Loved-ones also notice these and other changes. Whether the setting is in hospice facility, hospital, or at home, loved-ones grieve the day when a terminal loved-one takes his/her last breath. Yet what catches most people off-guard is the fact that anticipatory grief involves grieving not only the future, but also includes the present and past. We become aware of multiple layers of loss as we become attuned to what has been, what we are losing now and what we will not have in the future.

The way I awaken empathy in my clinical students regarding anticipatory grief is by having them participate in a group exercise. Each student makes a list of 20 things/

people that they cherish the most. In other words, *"if you were only allowed to possess 20 things/people in your life, what/who would they be?"* These items can include anything ranging from their faith to health, careers, favorite foods, to even bodily mobility and functions they take for granted, religious or spiritual practices, and significant people in their lives: loved-ones, mentors, neighbors, clubs, organizations, etc. Once the list is complete, students exchange their lists with a partner. The partner is then required to randomly cross out four items on the list — every two minutes. The author of the list, sits there quietly, journaling their inner reactions toward what is often interpreted later as "quite unfair!" As one student remarked:

I couldn't believe it! All I could do was sit there and watch somebody else erase decades of relationships, accomplishments, and memories. It was as if I was being erased. They had no regard for my feelings! I had no say! I was so angry and hurt, and there was nothing I could do to stop it!

Most of the students are shocked by their reactions. I imagine reading this exercise, you would be as well. In fact, many people would rather be in control of what they would cross off, than not being able to pick and choose which beloved relationships, items or bodily functions are taken from them. Yet, herein lays the cold truth of anticipatory grief: we often do not get the opportunity to pick and choose what we have to relinquish as a result of our failing bodies. In fact, if given the opportunity, I imagine we would never be ready to let go. However, the reality is that we suffer multiple losses before the actual, physical death of a loved-one. It's true. The moment people receive the news of a life-threatening illness or disease, they begin to grieve. But, this is only the beginning of several changes, losses and grief they will go through, and they do not wade through this process alone. Loved-ones and close friends also grieve many losses along the way. Some are losses of a <u>physical nature</u>: the loss of control over certain bodily functions, diminished appetite or inability to enjoy certain foods because they irritate the lining of our loved-one's stomach or intestines. Eyesight or hearing becomes weakened. Mobility decreases to the point where your loved-one may be required to use a foli bag or catheter to eliminate wastes. Their bodies grow weary and they may spend most of their time sleeping. Regarding <u>emotional</u> losses, our loved-ones may suffer from dementia, unable to recognize caregivers. There may be bouts of depression and anxiety over the feeling of not being in control of what is happening to them. Old wounds from harsh words once spoken between family members may resurface. As a result, the desire to reconcile may be overshadowed by stubborn pride.

For people and their families facing the end-stages of a terminal illness, but also wrestling with anticipatory grief, hospice offers a healthy way to address these issues. When most people think of hospice, what immediately comes to mind is a giving up or giving in to death. Nothing could be further from the truth! The hospice movement in the United States first began through the efforts of physician Dame Cicely Saunders, who began working with dying patients in the 1940's. Dr. Saunders founded the first modern hospice, St. Christopher's Hospice, in London, England. There, she not only worked to improve the quality of life in dying people by addressing the needs of care and pain management, but also sought to treat the dying with dignity and respect. Dr. Saunders came to believe and to teach, *"We do not have to cure to heal."* In my work I've been fortunate enough to see the positive impact hospice plays in the lives of the terminally ill and their families. From doctors, nurses and social workers to spiritual counselors/chaplains and volunteers, hospice provides multi-layered care to help meet the needs of patients and families.

Whether we are aware of our own mortality through being confronted with a diagnosis of a terminal illness, recognize the physical and mental limitations that come with the aging process, or compelled to say goodbye to loved-ones upon their death, grief is a normal reaction to such changes and losses. Grief is manifested in many ways and changes our perceptions about severed bonds we once held with each other. But this is only the beginning. If only our wounds could talk, what stories they could tell! Stories indeed. Every wound has a story behind it. Who we are, where we have been and what we have experienced. Mostly, our wounds reveal the truth about how much healing we have allowed in our lives, and how far we have yet to heal. Still, if we are faithful to this process of healing, we discover that in looking at our scars (emotional or otherwise), we can maintain our memories about life void of pain.

OUR SCARS

As children, we were always comparing our physical scars with our friends to see who among us earned their badges for courage. These scars would be the results of skinned knees from bicycle accidents, cuts on our arms from climbing trees, and even an occasional head on collision with a teammate on the baseball field. For example, whenever a friend showed us the scar on his leg he received while sledding last winter, we would quickly scan our bodies to see who could top that with the latest trip to the emergency room. Of course, there was always the kid who could silence us all just be lifting his shirt and showing off his scar from his appendectomy. Whatever they might be, our scars were proudly displayed for all to witness and admire our heroism.

Of course, this pastime is not limited to children. Adults too, sort of play this game at church picnics, family gatherings or whenever boredom takes over. Someone will usually begin by bragging about their latest injury during a long-overdue home project or who, among the women, had the most difficult caesarian delivery. But I believe there's a huge psychological difference between children showing off their battle-scars and when adults do so. Perhaps the reason is because adults want to illicit more sympathy from their peers than children. In the clinical field this attention-seeking behavior is called "secondary gains." In other words, people might derive some psychological benefit (e.g., sympathy, admiration, pity, etc.) from others when they point out how difficult their lives have been.

Classic and contemporary marriage and family therapists tell us that all families define acceptable ways for children to behave and offer them an emotional and practical definition of love. In fact, children come with a hard-wired need to feel loved and accepted. If this need is not met by the child's parents, caregivers, etc., he/she will fill the void with something else. This means that how we were treated as children and what kind of attention and reinforcement we were given, formulated our definition of love. As adults, sometimes our present dysfunctional behavior is part of a mixed up attempt to be loved in the terms of our histories.

In counseling others, I'm always struck by how people often "lead with their scars." By this I mean that a person's scars (physical or otherwise), have become an identity, a means by which he or she wants to be known by others, thereby often perpetuating an endless cycle of emotional victimization. Now don't get me wrong, compassion and empathy are two most important features we need to have for others. And of course, who are we to judge unless we've walked a mile in their shoes. Still, some people who have been through difficult ordeals don't know how to stop picking at their wounds. For one reason or another, a scab never forms on top of the wounds of physical and emotional abuse, sexual promiscuity, or even the death of a loved-one. More often than not, it's easy to spot this kind of behavior through initial impressions. Just pay attention to how people present themselves and/or how they describe their lives. For example, Josh, was a 30-something year old man who I counseled for *Post-Traumatic Stress Disorder* (PTSD). He was a rather large man with piercing green eyes and a three-inch scar across his left cheek from a knife wound. I remember the first time I met him in the waiting area of the counseling agency. As I introduced myself, he stood up with a glaring look. I'm sure his intention was meant to intimidate me. From the anxiety tightening across my chest, it must have worked. Within the first session, Josh told me the details of his trauma: One night as he was waiting for the subway, he was attacked by three men with knives. He remembered catching only a shadow of a person out of the corner of his eye. As he turned to see who it was, he was struck in the head with a blunt object, and a burning sensation on his face, causing him to fall down in a daze. He remembers being stabbed a couple of times before everything went black and waking up in the emergency room with a concussion and several lacerations. Although it had been two years since the attack, Josh's PTSD symptoms (startle response from loud noises and seeing shadows, uncomfortable around subways, sleepless nights, severe bouts of panic in crowded places, etc.) were never dealt with. In fact, they had begun to increase in their intensity along with his anti-anxiety medication, not to mention, every time he looked into the mirror, he was reminded of the attack. As we talked, it made sense to me, given his traumatic experience that he would "lead with his scars." Deep down inside he had secretly vowed that he would never feel that vulnerable again, and therefore, he would use his "scars" to intimidate others. It worked. He had successfully managed to isolate (and insulate) himself from others, especially strangers. During one session, Josh mentioned that he believed everything happened for a reason, but could not fathom why the attack happened to him. To him, attacking someone for a mere twenty dollars didn't make sense (this was how much money he had in his wallet). *"Besides the money, what else have they taken from you?"* I asked. You could have heard a pin drop. In fact, from the look of astonishment on his face, I swear I heard his heart break at that moment. As he tried to fight back the tears that were cemented behind his wall of trauma, his interior fortress was crumbling. In that moment he realized that he was allowing his attackers to take more than just twenty bucks. He also was allowing them to take away his peace of mind, his joy, his intimacy in relationships, etc. All the things he enjoyed about his life, he was surrendering to the scars of his past.

Josh started to understand, as do most people, that we sometimes unconsciously set ourselves up for a life of unhappiness by reinforcing our scars as a way to protect against potential, and often more painful, wounding by others. Within the logic of our internal defense mechanisms of denial, projection, displacement, regression, etc., we tell ourselves that we are making the best of a bad situation, beating others to the punch (perhaps literally), or even breaking our own hearts before anyone else can. Paradoxically, these tactics work: Our physical scars have the potential to remind us of the emotional wounds that have become encapsulated to keep the world out, and the pain in. The musical duo of Simon and Garfunkel once sang, *"And a rock feels no pain, and an island never cries."* The flip-side to this perspective is that people who isolate themselves also never take the risks of experiencing peace, love, joy, or any of the other positive emotions that remind us what it means to thrive and be fully human. John Donne (d. 1631), English Jacobean poet and preacher, makes this point even clearer when he wrote:

"All mankind is of one author, and is one volume; when one man dies, one chapter is not torn out of the book, but translated into a better language; and every chapter must be so translated...As therefore the bell that rings to a sermon, calls not upon the preacher only, but upon

the congregation to come: so this bell calls us all: but how much more me, who am brought so near the door by this sickness....No man is an island, entire of itself... any man's death diminishes me, because I am involved in mankind; and therefore never send to know for whom the bell tolls; it tolls for thee."
(Devotions upon emergent occasions and several steps in my sickness - Meditation XVII, 1624)

Whereas grief is the initial, subjective, and multi-faceted reaction to any loss, specifically, the reaction to the death of a loved one, mourning is best understood as the longer term process of adapting to the loss of the relationship. This is where the majority of grief work is done. An initial criticism by Rando (1993) is:

Many caregivers assist those who mourn with the beginning process (i.e., expressing their reactions to the loss), but not with the important later processes (i.e., reorienting in relation to the deceased, the self, and the external world). As a result, mourners are frequently left on their own to reshape self and world after the loss of a loved one (p.22).

Summary Paradigms of Loss and Grief

I remember the first time I went on a roller-coaster. I was about 9 years old. Part of my excitement stemmed from not knowing what would happen next. Buckled in my seat, the rush of anticipation would race through the passengers as the ride would be pulled up, up, up toward the top of the first, and often steepest climb. At the time I was too young to appreciate Oscar Wilde's quote: *"The suspense is terrible - I hope it lasts."* Then, without warning, the cars would swoosh down a steep slope, and then make a sharp turn with a jerk. From that point on, the best you could do was to hang on, often for dear life! The fun was being jostled and bounced around in your seat. Now that I'm several decades older, I do not relish that out-of-control feeling. Instead, I much rather prefer rides that are predictable. I imagine the same thing is true with grief. We want to know what's coming up next for us, and despite the fact that millions of people watch "psych-thriller" movies, most people do not like to be frightened. Doka and Martin (2000) also use the analogy of a roller coaster for grief work. When we experience a loss we often find ourselves on an up-and-down cycle, sometimes over-whelmed by the loss. The energy generated by that tension may wax and wane as they continue to redefine life in the presence of loss. This cycle tends to be more intense in the first two years; after that, generally the low points become less intense, are experienced less often, and do not last as long. Over time most bereaved persons experience an ame-lioration, or improvement, of their grief symptoms.

Grief paradigms help us make sense of our losses by helping us place our experiences into an objective context in order to learn from them. This is certainly true from the standpoint of grief and mourning. Historically, the mourning process often has been described as stages, phases, or tasks (Worden, 2008). Psychological, physical and even religious/spiritual criteria have set the parameters for identifying how well a person is adapting to the death of a loved one. However, public opinion often mistakenly believes that the more quickly people pass through these sign-posts, the better they are in getting on with their lives. This concept is not necessarily the case for everyone. These criteria are not hurdles to be overcome once and for all, but are more fluid indicators to help people work through their change, loss, and grief. Despite the criteria for identifying how well a person works through his/her grief, mourning is a long-term process. Klass, et al. (1996) notes that although the intensity of feelings may lessen over time, the belief that the bereavement process ends at a determined point for everyone does not fit most people's experiences. For example, most of the emphasis on mourning is placed on letting go, instead of *"renegotiating the meaning of the loss over time. . .the process does not end, but in different ways bereavement affects the mourner for the rest of his or her life"* (p. 19). Still, debate among clinicians continues regarding the appropriate length of time needed to mourn, ranging from a little as 2 months to as much as 2 years (Corr, Nabe, and Corr, 2003).

Mourning as a Mental Task:

Sigmund Freud in his famous work *Mourning and Melancholia* (1917) proposed that grief required a person to perform a very distinct mental task, i.e., a *cathexis*, or a release of mental energy holding an object or person. When the "object" of our love ceased to exist (e.g., mother, father, etc.), the person became conscious of the loss, and the emotional attachment (libido) would then be required to withdraw that energy from the deceased person/object. I like to think of Freud's concept as a burned-out light-socket. Whatever you plug into the socket will not work, because there's no electricity being supplied to run your lights or other appliances. Therefore, it only makes sense to find another outlet that supplies electrical current. Freud's work helped researchers begin to understand that mourning was and is a process, a working through the loss of a loved-one. An example of this *cathexis* might be when a widow/widower starts to date or marries again. She/he may still have feelings for the deceased spouse, but has reconnected their emotional and physical energies into a new relationship(s).

Unresolved grief and psychosomatic illness

As previously mentioned, Eric Lindemann's (1944) initial work with acute grief reactions was also ground-breaking in terms of how unresolved grief is a factor in many psychosomatic illnesses. In a paper presented to the Massachusetts Psychiatric Society in February 1942, Lindemann noted that the psychiatric treatment for ulcerative colitis centered around the problem of helping mourning patients achieve the readjustment necessitated by the loss of a loved one. Later that year, the Coconut Grove Nightclub caught fire and killed 492 people. Lindemann, observing the grief reactions of those who lost loved ones in this fire, saw similar psychosomatic characteristics resulting from mourning a beloved person. These observations led Lindermann (1986) to formulate three stages of grief work: (1) emancipation from the bondage to the deceased, (2) readjustment to the environment in which the deceased is missing, and (3) the formation of new relationships. Today when I'm counseling people who recently have lost a loved-one, it is not uncommon for me to ask if they have been to their primary care physician for a physical. What I have discovered is that most people do not understand how we often hold our sadness and pain in our bodies, albeit in the form headaches, ulcers, back pain, or other somatic symptoms. Once physical origins for symptoms are either ruled out or treated, I encourage people to address their emotional, psychological and spiritual issues to assimilate their losses in their present lives.

Kübler-Ross' stages of grief

Elizabeth Kübler-Ross (2007), working first with dying patients and then with bereaved people, understood a person's experience in dealing with death in five stages. The first stage is *Shock and Denial,* in which patients appear dazed at first when they receive news of their illness or loss and may deny that anything is wrong. Second, there is *Anger*, often manifested as frustration, irritability, blame, or hostility at themselves, doctors, caregivers, and even family members. The third stage is *Bargaining*, which involves an attempt to negotiate with friends, caregivers, or God. An example of this stage might be how people believe in return for a cure, they promise to live better lives or promise to fulfill a pledge or another neglected obligation. Fourth, there is *Depression* during which patients show signs of clinical depression, such as emotional withdrawal, sleep and eating disturbances, and possibly, suicide ideation. The last stage is *Acceptance*, in which the person realizes that death or loss is inevitable, and he/she accepts the finality of the experience. At this stage many people find themselves ready to "let go." Despite the popularity of the stage approach, Worden (2008) agrees with Kübler-Ross in that a major limitation of "stages" is that people do not pass through them in a neat, sequential order. Many times, people who mourn fluctuate among the stages before coming to acceptance. For example, it is not uncommon for a person who is in end stages of a terminal illness to be filled with anger and rage one day, and the next day slip into depression, only to experience the anger all over again the next day or next week.

Mourning process as phases

Another approach to understanding the mourning process is through phases. Both Parkes (1972) and Bowlby (1980) define four phases of mourning: *Phase One* (Numbing) is the period of numbness occurring close to the time of the loss, which may last from a few hours to a few weeks, and may or may not be accompanied by outbursts of distress and anger. *Phase Two* (Protest), a period of yearning and searching occurs as the survivor longs to be reunited with the deceased and denies the permanence of the loss. *Phase Three* (Despair), as the hope of recovery fades, and when the bereaved person finds it difficult to function in everyday life, thereby experiencing a period of disorganization and despair. In *Phase Four* (Reorganization) persons begin to detach emotionally from the relationship, seek new relationships, and reorganize their behavior in everyday activities.

Mourning as task completion

The understanding of mourning as "phases" is also criticized by Worden (2008), in that it implies passivity on the part of the survivor as he or she passes through phases. Thus, Worden's understanding of the mourning process emphasizes the "Tasks" concept, and asserts that the mourner needs to take action or to do something. Worden's *Four Tasks of Mourning* include: (1) *Accept* the reality of the loss, intellectually and emotionally; (2) *Experience* the pain of grief without trying to suppress painful memories; (3) *Adjust* to an environment in which the deceased is missing; and (4) *Form* new attachments, by finding a psychological place for the deceased that will enable the mourner to be connected, in a way that will not prevent him/her from going on with life. Within this paradigm, the third task involves an external adjustment (interpersonal), in which a survivor adapts to different things, people, roles, and relationships. There is also an internal adjustment (intrapersonal) whereby the survivor must adapt to his/her own sense of self; self-definition, self-esteem, and self-efficacy.

Doka (2002) proposes a "fifth task" to Worden's paradigm: *Rebuild* faith and philosophical assumptions that have been challenged by the loss. A major obstacle for many people in assimilating their grief is to reexamine their core beliefs about how life "ought to" operate. From when we were young, our lives are built upon assumptions about how the world should work, when and how God should act, matters of faith and obedience, rewards and punishment, etc. Ironically, most of these assumptions about life come to us in the form of fairy tales. Although they are loved and cherished by young and old, they nevertheless involve some intensely painful and dark experiences. For example, overcome by her jealousy of Snow White, the wicked witch devises a plan to kill her and convinces others she has succeeded. However, in the end she meets her doom at the hands of Prince Charming. Likewise, Cinderella's step mother and sisters, treat her cruelly, and break her heart by not allowing her to go to the ball.

By the end of the story, the wicked step-mother and step-sisters plans unravel and Cinderella and the prince live happily ever after. When we experience the pain of losing a loved-one to death, our unchallenged assumptions about life, fairness in the world, even the goodness of God, often muddy the waters of the process of mourning. Unconsciously, we may wonder why we are not allowed to "live happily ever after" with our spouses, or question what it is we have done that God is punishing us for? However the truth is that death and dying are a part of life and living. Hopefully, the awareness of our mortality awakens us to become better, not bitter, persons of faith.

Rando's six "r's" in mourning

Therese A. Rando (1993) emphasizes the six "R's" for processing one's mourning: (1) Recognize the loss; (2) React to the separation; (3) Recollect and re-experience the deceased and the relationship; (4) Relinquish the old attachments to the deceased and the old assumptive world; (5) Readjust to move adaptively into the new world without forgetting the old; and (6) Reinvest in life. Rando also notes that if survivors of death-related losses do not work through this process of mourning, they have a tendency to do two things, which "complicate" their mourning. They may deny, repress, and/or avoid aspects of the loss, its pain, and the full realization of its implications for the mourner. Secondly, they may hold onto, and avoid relinquishing, the lost loved one. These complications may in turn create increased levels of depression, elevated anxiety, and may reinforce maladaptive ways of coping, e.g. through alcohol or drug abuse.

Grief reactions: normal and complicated

Grief is considered a "normal" reaction to any type of loss, and can be experienced on many different levels. There is, however, a point when grief is considered abnormal. This phenomenon occurs when grief and mourning become complicated as the level of impairment escalates to the point of severely limiting the day-to-day functioning of one who mourns a loss.

From a cognitive perspective, Neimeyer et al. (2002) suggests that complicated grief occurs when a person is unable to assimilate the loss into his/her personal life narrative. In other words, *"reconstruct a meaningful personal reality"* (p. 236) by relearning assumptions about the world, roles in the family, etc., challenged by the loss.

Lazare (1979) suggests that abnormal, or pathological, grief occurs when one or more of the following symptoms are evident: (1) when a person is not able to talk about the deceased without experiencing a fresh grief reaction; (2) when minor events trigger an intense emotional response; (3) when the death of the loved one is often the topic of conversation; (4) when there is a reluctance to remove the loved one's possessions; (5) when the survivor reports physical symptoms similar to those of the deceased's; (6) when a

survivor has made radical and sudden lifestyle changes following the loss; or (7) when the survivor becomes preoccu-
pied with the presence of the deceased.

Catalan (1995) affirms that pathological grief can be categorized under several headings. *Absence or delayed grief*
is an absence or delay of the manifestations of numbness
and disbelief, separation distress, and subsequent features
associated with normal grief. *Chronic grief* occurs when
the most distressing features of mourning persist over time,
and the intensity of emotions escalate as well. For example,
although anniversary reactions to the death of a loved one
are considered normal, even after many years, a person still
may feel unable to move on with their lives, or complain
about being "stuck" in their grief (Worden, 2008). *Inhibited
or distorted grief* is seen in people with an erratic pattern
of emotional responses and thoughts. Complaints of somatic
symptoms, anxiety, depression, or behavioral manifestations
such as hostility, displaced anger, and over-identification
with the deceased may become more prominent than the
usual features of mourning.

The fourth edition of the Diagnostic and Statistical
Manual (DSM-IV, 1994) provides therapists with guidelines
regarding the context of bereavement. Listed as V62.82,
bereavement is the category assigned to a person who
exhibits a reaction to the loss of a loved one. As part of this
reaction to the loss, some people display symptoms associated with Major Depressive Episode (e.g., feelings of sad-

ness, insomnia, poor appetite, fatigue, weight loss, etc.). Yet, in order to differentiate between bereavement and Major Depressive Episode, the clinician is urged to note the duration, i.e., *if the symptoms persist for longer than two months, or are characterized by marked functional impairment, morbid preoccupation with worthlessness, suicide ideation, psychotic symptoms, or psychomotor retardation* (p.684).

Many clinicians, including myself, believe that the DSM-IV criteria for a bereavement diagnosis is quite unrealistic in light of the on-going research in the field of grief, mourning and bereavement (Hartz, 1986; Parkes and Weiss, 1983; Rando, 1993; and Houck, 2007). For example, such criticism includes unrealistic expectations regarding the duration of what is considered to be "normal" bereavement, the lack of criteria for specific populations of bereaved individuals (bereaved parents, siblings, death of parents, spouses, life partners, and children) and expanding the symptom criteria of grief to include separation anxiety. As a result of inadequate criteria, Rando (1993) notes that *"caregivers are forced to assign other diagnoses that have clinical implications unacceptable to many bereaved individuals. Common diagnoses include one of the depressive, anxiety, or adjustment disorders; brief reactive psychosis; or one of the other V-code diagnoses"* (pg.13).

The future of bereavement research

An area of research that has gained attention in the field of bereavement is the merging of two disciplines, i.e., thanatology and traumatology. In the past, bereavement issues have been understood and treated exclusively in terms of depression (Rando, 2000). Although depressive symptoms are part of grief, anxiety and traumatic stress symptoms often have been overlooked as critical factors in the early stages of grief and, therefore, left untreated at the expense of focusing on depressive symptoms.

Traumatic grief

One direction the merging of thanatology and traumatology has taken is in the Traumatic Grief criteria proposed by Jacobs (1999).

Criteria A

Person has experienced the death of a significant other
The response involves intrusive, distressing
preoccupation with the deceased person
(e.g., yearning, longing, or searching)

Criteria B

Frequent efforts to avoid reminders of the deceased
(e.g., thoughts, feelings, activities, people, places).
Purposelessness or feelings of futility about the future.

Subjective sense of numbness, detachment, or
absence of emotional responsiveness.
Feeling stunned, dazed, or shocked.
Difficulty acknowledging the death (e.g., disbelief).
Feeling that life is empty or meaningless.
Difficulty imagining a fulfilling life without the deceased.
Feeling that part of oneself has died.
Shattered world view (e.g., lost sense of
security, trust, or control).
Assumes symptoms or harmful behaviors of,
or related to, the deceased person.
Excessive irritability, bitterness, or anger
related to the death.

Criteria C
The duration of the disturbance is at least two months

.

Criteria D
The disturbance causes clinically significant
impairment in social, occupational, or other important
areas of functioning.

Embedded in Bowlby's Attachment Theory (1980), sep-aration anxiety occurs when a bereaved person experiences the pang of grief and engages in searching behavior in an attempt to recover the relational bond between himself/her-self and the deceased. Jacobs states that *"while there is evi-*

dence for a higher risk of Major Depression during acute bereavement, there is also evidence for a higher risk of anxiety disorders and Posttraumatic Stress Disorder (PTSD)" (p.14). His rationale for including stress-related disorders is because "a death can be inherently traumatic (especially if sudden and/or violent) and fundamentally shake the assumptions about a secure life and future attachments of the bereaved survivor" (pg. 19).

A major criticism of the Jacobs' Traumatic Grief criteria is that it requires a person to experience the death of a significant other. *"Losses other than death, such as loss of a home, loss of job, divorce, loss of limb, or loss of health, do not qualify for the diagnosis"* (p.28). Although the majority of bereavement research and literature focuses on the death of persons, other types of losses (actual and/or potential threat) support a more inclusive understanding of bereavement issues (Rando, 1993; Jeffreys, 1995; Nolen-Hoeksema and Larson, 1999). For example, I have counseled women following a mastectomy as part of their cancer treatment. They feel that having a significant part of themselves surgically removed was just as traumatic for them as losing a loved-one to death. As one woman explained to me, *"The part of me that showed others I was becoming a young woman is now gone."* Other people who have had a leg removed due to advanced diabetes also struggle with the emotional trauma of adjusting to losing a major part of themselves to an illness. Children, adolescents, and adults regardless of age and gender, who are survivors of violent acts such as incest, rape, assault and other emotional/physical/spiritual abuses would more than likely agree that their experiences were very traumatic for them. In fact, it is not uncommon for these survivors to have suffered years under the weight of shame, guilt, fear of being humiliated, low self-esteem, self-harming behaviors, sexual misconduct, etc.

Traumatic bereavement

Although Rando (2000) acknowledges the merging of loss and trauma, she believes that bereavement is more than merely the sum of these two experiences. In fact, within the interaction of loss and trauma, a new and different entity is created, i.e., *traumatic bereavement* (p.173). She identifies six high-risk factors that have the potential for making any death traumatic for the bereaved:

Rando's Traumatic Bereavement Criteria
Suddenness of death and lack of anticipation
Violence, mutilation, and destruction
Preventability and randomness
The loss of a child
Multiple deaths
The mourner's personal encounter with death, secondary to either a significant threat to survival, or a massive and/or shocking confrontation with death and the mutilation of others.

In studying children's responses to exposure to violent and traumatic deaths, Nader (1997) discovered four ways in which the interaction of grief and trauma may affect the bereavement process.

Nader's Interaction of Grief and Trauma

The interplay of grief and trauma may intensify the symptoms common to both
Thoughts of the deceased may lead to traumatic recollections
Traumatic aspects of the death may hinder or complicate issues of bereavement, such as grief dream work, relationship to the deceased, issues of identification, and processing of anger and rage
A sense of posttraumatic estrangement or aloneness may interfere with healing social interactions.

With the emergence of treating loss and grief issues as traumatic, mourning has moved in the direction from exclusively alleviating depressive symptoms, to having a more extensive knowledge of the interplay between loss, grief, anxiety, and trauma.

In summary, grief is a normal reaction to any experience (real or perceived) of a change or separation, which creates a sense loss. This reaction is especially relevant in the death of a loved one. Grief takes myriad expressive forms because no two people react the same way to loss. Nonetheless, as noted above, researchers, while disagreeing as to the specific form it takes, do agree that mourning occurs as a process in which survivors must come to terms with the reality of the death, express their emotions, and move on with the lives without the deceased. If this does not occur, grief can become encapsulated, resulting in further emotional, physical, and psychological problems for surviving loved-ones.

"Death ends a life, not a relationship." Tuesdays With Morie

Klass (1996) notes that although intense feelings of loss and grief may lessen over time, the belief that the mourning process ends at a determined point for everyone, does not fit most people's experiences. As previously mentioned, according to the *Diagnostic and Statistical Manual, fourth edition,* the diagnosis for Bereavement is not given unless the symptoms of grief, i.e., sadness, depression, insomnia, poor appetite, etc., are persistent after two months. Ironically, many people believe they should be over their loss prior to this time, if not shortly thereafter. In fact, quite often family members, friends, even co-workers might grow impatient when people still exhibit the signs of mourning weeks and months after a death. For many who have lost loved-ones to death, this expectation is simply absurd. As Nancy, a 78 year old widow told me, *"There's no way anyone can be over their loved-one's death after two months! I'm still trying to figure out how to return the casserole dishes to people who brought them to the wake!"* How true. Still, I've seen people place unnecessary pressure on themselves to hurry the mourning process along, in hopes that if they can just get rid of all signs of their loss, they can move on with life. This idea never works. Instead of dealing with the loss and working through the pain in healthy ways and on their own timetable, grief may become layered in our lives.

The fact is that nobody can dictate how long it will take for grief symptoms to dissipate. Rando (1993) list several "factors" which affect the intensity and duration of the mourning process:

PSYCHOLOGICAL FACTORS

Characteristics pertaining to the nature and meaning of the specific loss:
Unique nature and meaning of the loss sustained
or relationship severed
Qualities of the relationship lost, psychological character
strength, and security of the attachment
Role the deceased occupied in the mourner's
family or social system.
Characteristics of the deceased
Amount of unfinished business between the
mourner and the deceased

Mourner's perception of the deceased fulfillment in life
Number, type and quality of secondary losses
Nature of any on-going relationship with the deceased

Characteristics of the mourner:
Coping behaviors, personality, and mental health
Level of maturity and intelligence
Assumptions about the world
Previous life experiences, especially past experiences with
loss and death
Expectations about grief and mourning
Social, cultural, ethnical, generational, and religious/philo-
sophical/spiritual background
Sex-role conditioning and age
Developmental stage of life, life-style, and sense of
meaning and fulfillment
Presence of concurrent stresses or crises

Characteristics of the death:
The location of the death, type of death, reasons for it,
mourner's presence at it, degree of
confirmation of it, mourner's degree of
preparation and participation
Timeliness of the death
Psychosocial context within which the death occurs
Amount of mourner's anticipation of death
Degree of suddenness

Mourner's perception of preventability
Length of illness prior to the death
Amount, type, and quality of anticipatory grief and involvement with the dying person

SOCIAL FACTORS

Mourner's social support system and the recognition, validation, acceptance, and assistance provided by its members
Mourner's social, cultural, ethnical, generational, and religious/philosophical/spiritual background
Mourner's educational, economic, and occupational status
Funeral or memorial rites
Involvement in the legal system
Amount of time since the death

PHYSIOLOGICAL FACTORS:

Drugs (including alcohol, caffeine, and nicotine)
Nutrition
Rest and sleep
Exercise
Physical health

To this list I would certainly add:

RELIGIOUS/SPIRITUAL FACTORS

Involvement in one's community of faith;
attending services, volunteering, etc.
Level of support from faith community;
prayers, visitation, etc.
Specific religious rituals important to survivor's
well being; memorial services, etc.
Specific theological beliefs; after-life, sins,
forgiveness, karma, etc.

Depending on these above factors, I believe it is not uncommon for a person to mourn for a minimum of one to two years. The key is to remember that just as it takes time to get to know someone, it also takes time to let go. For example, Marie was widowed at age 56. She and her husband (Sam) of 32 years raised three beautiful daughters and shared lots of memories. When Sam died of Hodgkin's Disease two years ago, Marie came to me for counseling. One of the first things she asked me was if I knew anyone who wanted his things, i.e., all of his things. When I asked why this request seemed urgent, she explained that her friends told her she would feel better once she got rid of her husband's possessions. From the look on her face I could tell she did not believe her friends, so I asked her how she was feeling currently. She replied with a heavy sigh, *"Not so good."* Over 32 years of marriage she and Sam had acquired many things. Marie said she felt that if she got rid of the possessions, she was not only getting rid of his memory, but also she felt she was getting rid of parts of herself. I agreed. To help Marie through this process, I suggested that she get ten large cardboard boxes, and fill them with all the possessions she wanted to keep right now. She was then to store these boxes in her attic or basement for 3-6 months. The next time when she felt ready to go through the boxes again, she was to take away one box each time, and giving away or throwing out what she no longer wanted. When we met for counseling each time she would bring one of Sam's memories with her and a precious story to go along with it. I must admit that I looked forward to our sessions because of not only wondering what item she would bring next, but also watching her work through her grief from her stories. Sometimes she would laugh. Sometimes she would cry. All in all, little did she realize that she was being empowered to make her own decisions about her mourning process and her memories with Sam. The last time I checked with Marie, she was down to two boxes, which contained all the memories (photos, love letters, pins, postcards from vacations, etc.) she wanted to keep till the day she would die. I celebrated with Marie her ability to cherish her life with Sam. Oh and by the way, she feels much better these days.

Many people I've counseled have found comfort in knowing that it is normal to hold onto their loved-one's memories. Most of the literature on loss and grief emphasizes the need to let go, instead of reassuring the mourner about the *meaning* of the loss over time, i.e., that the process does not end, but in different ways, bereavement affects the person for the rest of his or her life (Klass, 2006). In fact, I am convinced that survivors who maintain a "continuing bond" with the deceased appear to be better adjusted psychologically and spiritually throughout their lives. For example, the bonds that were established between ourselves and our loved-ones are continuous. They assist us in dealing with on-going issues in life and are integrated into current relationships, providing them context and meaning. It's not uncommon for people to report dreaming of their loved-one or talking out loud to them as if they are still around. After my father's death I would often talk out loud to him, asking his advice or asking what he would think about this and such if he were around today. Crazy? Not in the least. In fact, I often feel better after having a long talk with him.

Another way people maintain the emotional bonds with their loved-ones is through wearing tangible objects such as a watch, carrying pictures in their wallets, or wearing some other kind of jewelry. Within the past years a new phenomena has also helped people maintain their connection all through the assistance of cell phones. Kaylee, a 17 year old girl who lost her father to cancer a year ago taught me something new about maintaining bonds. She said the family got permission to bury her father's cell phone at his graveside. As long as the phone bill is paid each month, the voicemail service remains active, even underground. Then, whenever she would like to hear her father's voice, she calls his number and leaves a long message. She said that during the first month she would call him every day. Now, she calls about every one to two weeks, just to say "hi, I miss you" and keep him informed about what's going on in her life. Cool.

One of the most precious stories I have ever heard about the emotional strength a person receives by maintaining the emotional bonds with a deceased loved-one comes from Barbara. Her husband John, of 41 years, was dying from pancreatic cancer. He was placed on hospice four months prior to his death. The hospice agency provided John and Barbara everything they needed: Nurses attended to his medication regimen and palliative care. The nurses' aides bathed John regularly and changed his dressings. The chaplain worked with their local minister, coordinating religious/spiritual support. But it was one particular volunteer who planted a simple seed of thoughtfulness that yielded an everlasting fruit in Barbara. Once a week this volunteer came to the house to sit with John as Barbara would spend the afternoon running errands. Over the course of time John shared stories of his life with the volunteer, who in her wisdom, wrote down every word and story in a journal. John talked about when he first met Barbara, and how nervous he was when he asked her to marry him. He shared stories about raising a family together, doctor visits and their special song. All this time the volunteer kept writing. Within the last few weeks of John's life he started to grow weaker and weaker. The stories were now fewer and farther in-between until he spent most his days sleeping. When there were no stories to write down from John, the volunteer sat quietly and wrote about her own feelings being with John during these moments. On the 3rd of November, John died. After the graveside service, the volunteer approached Barbara and handed her the journal she had written in over the past four months. Barbara thanked her for sitting with John and packed the journal away in some boxes when she arrived home. Thanksgiving seemed to come and go without Barbara ever noticing it. However, Christmas was going to be a different matter altogether, for it was John's favorite holiday. In 41 years they had never spent a Christmas apart. Barbara dreaded the thought of that Christmas being the first of many without John. On Christmas Eve, needless to say, Barbara did not feel like doing much of anything, let alone attending the many parties she was invited to. Instead, she remembered that she packed away the journal John's hospice volunteer gave her at the funeral. After finding the box that contained the journal, she made herself a cup of hot chocolate, lit her candles, turned on some soft Christmas music on the radio, wrapped herself in a wool blanket, and started to read the journal. Tears streamed down her cheeks as page after page carried her back over 41 years of shared memories. The day after Christmas, Barbara phoned the volunteer and thanked her for the wonderful gift of the journal. *"I couldn't have asked for a better Christmas!"* she said. *"It was as if John was right there with me. I even forgot some of those stories, but I will always cherish them. I miss him terribly, but for all of his pain and suffering he went through I would not want him back in that condition. I know he's in a better place."* So is she.

Throwing Salt in the Wounds: The Sting of Stigma

Although there are countless stories similar to Barbara and John's, there are other types of loss that stir such an uncomfortable feeling in society, that mourners do not feel they have the right to openly express their experiences. For example, throughout history certain diseases have carried a social stigma and have often struck fear and contempt into the hearts and lives of people around the world. Whether it was leprosy in early biblical times, tuberculosis (phthisis) in Ancient Greece, the Bubonic Plague in the Middle Ages, or the Acquired Immune Deficiency Syndrome (AIDS) in the late-twentieth century, societies have displayed a pattern of purposefully disenfranchising people who contracted these diseases. Initially, this reaction was justified as necessary in order to prevent the further spread of communicable diseases. However, many afflicted people interpreted being quarantined as society's way of displaying contempt for its sick. As a result, many felt stigmatized by their illness, shunned, and alienated from fully participating in their communities as persons of value and worth.

Goffman (1986) notes that the Greeks originated the term "stigma" to refer to bodily signs, designed to expose something unusual and negative about the moral status of the bearer. These "signs," imposed by society, were cut or burned into a person's body, advertising his/her condition, i.e., a slave, a criminal, or a traitor. As a result, this act of "branding" signified to all that the recipient was a blemished person, ritually polluted, and to be avoided. . .especially in public places. Such "markings" not only spoiled a person's social identity but also cut off that person from society, thus forcing him/her to live in isolation in an un-accepting world. From this aspect, it appeared as though there was no way to remove this outward sign, let alone recover from the emotional wounding from such harsh treatment.

While not always spoken, society clearly distinguishes between the so-called clean verses unclean, acceptable verses unacceptable, and lovable verses unlovable, people. Within disenfranchised grief, people living with certain diseases, e.g., HIV/AIDS, are often viewed with contempt for possibly contracting the disease through socially deviant behavior (sexual promiscuity, illegal intravenous drug use, prostitution, etc.). What I have discovered in counseling family members and friends, whose loved-ones died from an AIDS-related death, that upon their death, society's stigma is more than likely be transferred to their surviving loved-ones.

Therefore, despite its unpopularity it is crucial to give voice to the disenfranchised and embrace them as persons of value and worth.

Although a society's purity system was meant to impose "temporary" isolation, the practice eventually became an acceptable way to permanently expel people who "polluted" society by their conditions (Black, 1996). This expulsion was true not only for people who had an identifiable condition but also for those who had a condition that was not readily seen, such as mental illness. In today's society, not all the signs of socially intolerable disease are immediately visible, especially in the early stages of a person who has HIV/AIDS. However, once such a condition is disclosed, society's overall contempt for what is deemed as unacceptable behavior or flawed character reduces that person from a whole and unique individual, to a tainted, discredited one (Goffman, 1986). Corr (1998) notes that when a society imposes its stigma on a person, this ultimately leads to disenfranchisement, i.e., placing a person in a context in which he/she is not accorded the social right to have his/her voice heard or vote counted (p. 6). Such persons are confined to second-class status and political subjugation. On the other hand, Corr (1998) contends that to be "enfranchised" means a person enjoys the benefit of full admission to political freedom, a right and privilege extended by society to people who are at liberty to exercise participation in the affairs of the community.

Ironically, disenfranchisement not only happens to the discredited person with an unacceptable illness, but can also involve those who are close to the stigmatized individual. This disenfranchisement clearly has been seen within the context of HIV/AIDS. For example, Snyder, Omoto, and Crain (1999) observe a "guilt by association" judgment being rendered on loved ones, friends, caregivers, and can even extend to those who offer their services as volunteers to local HIV/AIDS agencies and causes. So, it seems that, while the symptoms of socially stigmatized diseases may remain less discernible for longer periods as medical expertise advances, the brush that marks persons with stigma, sweeps a much wider area. In other words, people living with stigmatized illnesses are not the only ones confronting social isolation.

Disenfranchised grief

The mark of marginalization can extend beyond death, even to those who mourn the death of a loved-one from a stigmatized disease. Because of their association with the deceased, survivors feel as though they cannot express their grief openly, but are forced to hide their feelings, thus exacerbating the painful process of mourning. They too, may view themselves as being "branded" by society as a result of loving another human being, whom society has discredited. For example, in the context of bereavement, Doka (2002) notes that there are specific losses that present a double-bind: While most people who mourn the loss of a loved one are free to experience normal grief reactions, others whose loved-ones carry social stigma are not given the right, role, or capacity to grieve as others may. Added to this, these mourners are given little or no social or religious support to help facilitate their grief (Doka, 2002).

Doka (2002) has postulated the reason for this reaction by society as arising from one or more of the following factors:

- *The relationship to the deceased is not recognized*, (e.g., homosexual relationship, divorced spouse, etc.) because it was not based on traditional kin ties.
- *The loss is not recognized*, or viewed by society as significant (e.g., loss of a pet, prenatal death).
- *The survivor is perceived by society as not having the capacity to mourn* (e.g., children, elderly).
- *There are certain types of death* (e.g., suicide and AIDS-related) which may be too embarrassing or produce heightened anxiety in members of society.

As previously mentioned, in both AIDS as well as suicide, the stigma (imposed by society's discomfort) is transferred to those who mourn the death of a loved one. Throughout history, the surviving loved-ones of a suicide were highly stigmatized, as many witnessed the deceased loved-one's body being drug through town, or put on display in the town as objects of ridicule and shame (Rubel, 2003).

Many bereaved families of a suicide had their land taken from them, and were forced to leave town. Places of worship would ban offering the sacrament of "Last Rights" to suicides, and would even refuse burial in sacred burial sites (Freedman, 1992). Even to this day, suicide can often be the "family secret," despite Western societies viewing suicide as a complex phenomenon associated with psychological, biological, and social factors (Corr, Nabe, & Corr, 2003).

In recent history, cancer was once a death that disenfranchised its grievers. Many people, out of fear of being perceived as flawed themselves, would whisper the name "cancer" when asked how a loved-one died. Sometimes, if a person's behavior (excessive smoking, drinking, etc.) contributed to the diagnosis of cancer and subsequent death, family members would be reluctant to share details, as it might be reflective on them (Corr, Nabe, & Corr, 2003). Nowadays, cancer is a relatively acceptable diagnosis and death. There are numerous support groups for bereaved loved-ones, and different ways to memorialize a loved-one through donations, charity golf outings, and benefit walks.

What is key to understanding disenfranchisement as it pertains to the subject of loss and bereavement is that it is always founded on a specific set of normative social attitudes and values (Corr, 1998). Doka (2002) notes that every society has norms that frame grieving. These rules dictate who, when, where, how, for how long, and for whom, people should grieve a loss. Such rules can have implications for a variety of instances, such as who is permitted to make funeral arrangements, attend memorial and funeral services, and company policies that determine bereavement leave to employees. These norms may serve to reinforce a feeling of isolation for a person who is disenfranchised in his/her grief. Again, I believe there is a truth worth repeating: While the definition of stigma and taboo can vary according to one culture, grief is universal: A normal, human reaction when a loved-one dies. Much in the same way every human being has a thumbprint, grief is the common denominator in all societies.

Religious and Spiritual scars

In such cases, the loss of religious and spiritual beliefs may add another dimension to disenfranchised grief. As previously mentioned, disenfranchised grief (Doka, 2002) is a phenomena in which a person has experienced the death of a loved one, but is not accorded the right to grieve based on one of these factors: the way a person grieves, the nature of the loss, the relationship to the deceased, or the uncomfortable nature of the death itself (e.g., AIDS, suicide). With the additional loss of one's religious and/or spiritual beliefs, people may discover they have become separated from both religious rituals and the community of faith, which could possibly provide them comfort and support (Doka and Morgan, 1993).

I remember sitting with other clergy at a seminar on ministering to the specific religious/spiritual needs of the HIV/AIDS community. Matthew, a 35 year old caterer, shared about how his life had been affected by the many friends and loved-ones he lost to the disease.

Not only had he mentioned the multiple layers to his grief as he mourned approximately eleven friends within one year, but also he talked about how his faith changed. He was a devout member of his faith community, faithfully attending weekly services, serving on various committees, and often filled in as liturgist. Although I admired his devotion to God and his church, what Matthew said next will always remind me just how devastating disenfranchisement can be to those who grieve. Through his tears he blurted out, "*I love my church, but through it all I've realized that my church doesn't love me!*" The lump in my throat quickly lodged in my stomach. He said that what wounded him the most was that when his fellow parishioners discovered who he associated with, and the fact that he was also HIV positive, the very place he looked to for solace, turned its back on him. The very place where he thought he could be free to embrace expressions of God's mercy, grace and unconditional love, became the very place where he experienced emotional coldness, cruelty and judgment.

Too often people who have experienced loss, grief, mourning and bereavement go through life in search of healing and grace. Instead of feeling drawn to communities of faith, people feel alienated by their wounds and ashamed of their scars. As they stare at the "All Are Welcome" signs that hangs over the entrance of places of worship, they know that acceptance comes with conditions: Conditions of appropriate circumstances, relationships and status. And communities of faith wonder why they keep seeing a decrease in their membership and weekly attendance? Talk about insanity! *Doing the same things over and over again expecting different results.* Perhaps the answers lie in the way communities of faith treat their "wounded." From a pastoral approach, communities of faith should awaken to the fact that they are most effective when they care for the wounded and scarred souls of society. In doing so, people are transformed when they experience tangible holiness through a very simple, yet powerful act of *redemption.*

OUR REDEMPTION

"The first step to healing is not to step away from the pain, but to step toward it. To face the anguish and living through it is the way of healing. But I cannot do that on my own. I need someone to keep me standing in it, to assure me that there is peace beyond the anguish, life beyond the death, and love beyond fear."   Henri Nouwen (Life in the Beloved)

My first understanding of redemption came in the form of *S&H Greenstamps®*. Between the 1930's to the late 1980's, *S&H Greenstamps®* were every bit as part of the American culture as apple pie and baseball. Retail stores and shops issued these stamps to people based on the amount of their purchase. Let's say, for example, that you bought fifty dollars worth of groceries. At the checkout, you would receive the amount of stamps equivalent to your purchase. The stamps would then be pasted in collector books, which would later be used to exchange for other household items. Instead of paying cash for an item, like a blender or sporting equipment, you would "redeem" your coupon books by applying them to the cost of the item.

Long before the folks at *S&H Greenstamps®* came up with the idea of trading stamps, the subject of *redemption* has been impacting people's lives for centuries. In fact, *redemption* is a major theological theme woven throughout Scripture. It appears more than 130 times in the Old Testament; 20 times in the New Testament. In both sections, *redemption* epitomizes the idea of one who has been rescued, delivered and released from all kinds of disenfranchisement: slavery, famine, poverty, disease, social injustices, oppression, and stigmatization. In one sense, to be redeemed also meant to be restored to a previous status, i.e., prior to a person's unfortunate circumstance. Yet what makes *redemption* powerful is the effect it has on people's lives. It not only gave them comfort and healing from their past, but also instilled hope for their future, empowering them to live in wholeness again.

Redemption in the Old Testament

A classic example of personal redemption appears in the Book of Ruth where an unnamed kinsman-redeemer had the responsibility to protect the social and financial interests of his extended family. Such duties included providing an heir for a brother who had died (Deuteronomy 25:5-10), buying back land that had been sold by a poor relative to another outside the family (Leviticus 25: 25-28), setting free a relative that had been sold into slavery (Leviticus 25: 47-49), and/or acting as an avenger against a person who killed your relative (Numbers 35: 19-21). Ruth's own story of redemption began as she and her mother-in-law Naomi were recent widows. In those days, widows and orphans were especially vulnerable to societal cruelties because they had no immediate family to protect or provide for them. So in her emptiness, Naomi urges her daughters-in-law to remain in Moab, while she decides to return to her people. But Ruth replies, *"Don't urge me to leave you or to turn back from you. Where you go I will go and where you stay I will stay. Your people will be my people and your God will be my God."* (Ruth 1:16) As a result, both Naomi and Ruth return to the land of Judah. Once settled, Naomi receives news that she has a relative on her husband's side named Boaz. As Boaz learned of Naomi and Ruth's circumstances, he offered to "redeem" them by buying all of the property of Naomi's husband and sons, as well as marrying Ruth. In this way he provided for Naomi and Ruth and preserved Elimelech's family line.

The understanding of redemption was also significant in Israel's relationship with God. In the Book of Leviticus, there were specific laws (chapters 11-27) given to the Israelites that guarded against people taking advantage of the disenfranchised. These laws were often referred to as the Holiness Code. The Code served as instructions for the people to maintain their holiness before God and one another. According to these laws, holiness was a condition which permeated all aspects of life. From birth to death, life was governed by maintaining a distinction between the holy and the profane, or between the clean and unclean. As Wenham (1979) notes, cleanliness was understood as the normal condition of most things and persons, and therefore, spiritual holiness was symbolized by physical perfection. Anything else, e.g., death, sickness, disease, coming in contact with bodily discharges, blood, etc., was considered a deviation of this norm. When people violated this code directly or indirectly, they were separated for a period of time from the community to avoid further contamination. For example, since the Israelites were forbidden to come in contact with blood, (because blood contained the life of a person) a woman was considered "ceremonially unclean" each month during her menstruation. This rule also included being separated from the community for a certain amount of time after she had given birth to her child (Leviticus 12:1-8). Depending on whether she gave birth to a son or daughter, also determined the amount of time she not only remained separate from her community, but also how long she was forbidden to touch any sacred objects or enter the sanctuary to worship God. Whatever she touched in her unclean state also became defiled. Likewise, matters of sickness and disease also rendered people ceremonially unclean. (Leviticus 13-15) Until the conditioned improved, people who suffered infectious diseases were isolated from their community. Typically, this involved about one week. In this isolated state, just as with the rules that applied to women during their menstruation, any object that came in contact with the infectious person also became unclean, and had to be washed or destroyed. If other people touched the unclean object on purpose or by accident, they also became unclean and were required to perform ceremonial washing. As previously mentioned in *Our Scars,* by today's standards some might consider these purity laws, which not only categorized people and objects as clean or unclean, but also banished people from the community, as being extreme. Yet what needs to be emphasized here was that a state of uncleanliness was temporary. Although God demanded holiness in everyday life, He never abandoned the people. Provisions were made in these laws for people to be redeemed from their unclean conditions and be welcomed back into the camp. For example, once the person's condition, say from an infectious disease, had returned to normal or enough time had elapsed, the person would be readmitted to the community by having the priest pronounce him/her "clean," and specific sacrifices were then offered to complete the ritual of purification.

Redemption in Christ's ministry

By the time of the first century C.E., the practice of temporarily quarantining unclean people became an acceptable way to expel them. . .permanently. This behavior was justified by the perception that unclean people somehow polluted the rest of society by their conditions (Black, 1996). Therefore, it was quite common for people who had leprosy to live in their own colony outside a town. To survive they had to beg for food and clothing, all from a distance lest the wind would blow their uncleanliness onto the townsfolk, or a passer-by. This expulsion was true not only for people who had an identifiable condition but also for those who had a condition that was not readily seen, such as mental illness. Similar to leprosy, mentally ill people were either forced to live in isolation or with like-conditioned people.

With the coming of Christ, redemption takes on a new meaning because it was now God who sought out those who were disenfranchised (leprous, sickened, diseased, social deviants, etc.) from the community and healed them. Instead of operating according to the confines of the Levitical purity laws, which forbid coming in contact with people who were disenfranchised, Christ's ministry was characterized by redeeming people under the theology of the Year of Jubilee (Leviticus 25, NIV). For example, Jesus revealed to others that his ministry of redemption was the fulfillment of the prophecy of Isaiah 61:1 as recorded in Luke 4:18-19 (NIV),

The Spirit of the Lord is upon me for God has appointed me to preach good news to the poor. God has sent me to proclaim that captives will be released, that the blind will see, that the downtrodden will be freed from their oppressors, and that the acceptable year of the Lord's favor had come.

In Isaiah 61:1, from which Jesus was quoting, the Hebrew word for "release/returned" is the same word used in Leviticus 25:10 (NIV),

Consecrate the fiftieth year and proclaim liberty throughout the land to all its inhabitants. It shall be a jubilee for you; each one of you is to return to his family property and each to his own clan.

From this usage, it seems likely that Isaiah's description of the "acceptable year of the Lord" was inspired by the jubilee year, which was a time when people and property would be restored to their original status. Thus it was the messianic age that brought liberty to the disenfranchised. Christian theologians (Moltmann, 1993, Wenham, 1979) affirm that this age began with Christ's first coming (Luke 4:21, NIV) and will be completed by his second coming (Luke 16:19-31 NIV). Therefore, the jubilee not only looks back to God's first redemption of the Israelites from their slavery in Egypt (Leviticus 25:38,55 NIV) but also looks forward to the restitution of all things (Acts 3:21; 2 Peter 3:13, NIV) (Wenham, 1979).

For me, the beauty of the gospel centers on how Christ viewed the woundedness of people. He never saw them as "sinners" but rather "lost." He never reduced people to their illness, disease, or situation in life, but instead, saw them as people in need of liberation. For faith communities today, and as a model for pastoral counseling, Christ's way of redemption is essential for those who desire to offer healing to the bereaved, disenfranchised or otherwise. This model of redemption, views Christ as one, who was in some ways, disenfranchised himself, because he did not conform to societal expectations and norms (Meier, 1994). Instead, he spoke out against the way the religious authorities misinterpreted the Levitical purity laws that kept afflicted people at a distance and marginalized, all for the sake of maintaining religious purity. In order to redeem such disenfranchised people, Christ went beyond the limits of the purity laws, reaching out to the "unclean" people on the fringes of society and restored them as persons of dignity and worth. By ministering to marginalized people, Christ enfranchised people as members of a far greater society, the Kingdom of Heaven. As the Apostle Paul writes:

In him we have redemption through his blood, the forgiveness of sins, in accordance with the riches of God's grace that he lavished on us with all wisdom and understanding. And he made known to us the mystery of his will according to his good pleasure, which he purposed in Christ, to be put into effect when the times will have reached their fulfillment—to bring all things in heaven and on earth together under one head, even Christ. (Ephesians 1:7-10)

However, unlike green stamps, whose worth was equivalent to the money spent, biblical redemption places more emphasis on a person being restored beyond that initial starting place in life. They were redeemed to far greater place or status in the eyes of heaven. In other words, a person's stigma was not only removed, but for many, redemption was their only hope of survival. For example, if you're like me you cannot wait to be reunited with your loved ones in heaven. After you've spent a thousand years or so catching up with long-lost loved ones, I imagine there are other people you might like to meet. Perhaps you would also like to meet Peter and ask him what it was like to walk on water? Maybe you want to meet Rahab and ask her what it sounded like when the Israelites marched around Jericho, blowing their trumpets and singing? For me, the person I want to meet is recorded in Luke 8:40-48 (NIV).

Now when Jesus returned, a crowd welcomed him, for they were all expecting him. Then a man named Jairus, a ruler of the synagogue, came and fell at Jesus' feet, pleading with him to come to his house because his only daughter, a girl of about twelve, was dying. As Jesus was on his way, the crowds almost crushed him. And a woman was there who had been subject to bleeding for twelve years, but no one could heal her. She came up behind him and touched the edge of his cloak, and immediately her bleeding stopped.

"Who touched me?" Jesus asked. When they all denied it, Peter said, "Master, the people are crowding and pressing against you." But Jesus said, "Someone touched me; I know that power has gone out from me." Then the woman, seeing that she could not go unnoticed, came trembling and fell at his feet. In the presence of all the people, she told why she had touched him and how she had been instantly healed. Then he said to her, "Daughter, your faith has healed you. Go in peace."

No, it's not Jarius. The person I want to meet is the woman who had suffered with the chronic issue of blood. Ironically, her story is mentioned briefly, nestled among Jarius' plea with Jesus to heal his daughter. Her story always reminds me that we often receive more than what we dare ask from the Lord because He wants us to have something better. That day, there was somebody else who was just as desperate as Jarius! For twelve long years this woman suffered with this chronic illness, and I guarantee you that these were the loneliest years of her life! Remember, the Jewish law declared that for as long as a woman had a bodily discharged of blood, she was ceremonially unclean. This meant that she had to stand outside the temple with the gentiles. She was not welcome to worship with the other women of her faith community. For twelve years she was cut off because of her illness, and yet, something inside of her wanted to risk being shamed again by others that day. That day she reached out to Jesus. Even today, stigmatized people still seek healing from their emotional wounds and scars when they reach out to helping professions.

Perhaps she heard rumors of Jesus; reports of him healing the sick and casting out demons. Maybe she overheard Jesus was coming through her town? Perhaps she thought he was the only one who could help her. With this in mind, the woman worked her way through the crowd. She could see all the people around Jesus, trying to push their way through. Everyone seemed to be in a hurry. As she got closer, she reached out her hand and touched the hem of his garment. And when she did, she experienced something she had not felt in twelve years. Perhaps it was a surge of electricity or a tingling rush as the issue of blood ceased. Either way, she experienced the power of God in the Son of God! That day, she experienced more than what she asked for: She was physically healed, set free from her emotional stigma and redeemed to take hold of a more fulfilling life!

As I reflect on this story, I often wonder that this woman could have touched Jesus anywhere. She could have touched his arm, shoulder or even gotten face to face with Jesus the way Jarius did. Instead, she touched the hem of his garment. I like to believe that what this woman actually touched was one of the tassels attached to the corners of Jesus' prayer shawl. You see, these tassels were more than a decorative flare to one's garment; they were actually a sign of God's promises. In Numbers 15:37-41 (NIV), God instructed the

Israelites to sew a blue cord on each tassel on the corners of their garments, to remind them that the God they serve is faithful to them.

> *The LORD said to Moses, "Speak to the Israelites and say to them: 'Throughout the generations to come you are to make tassels on the corners of your garments, with a blue cord on each tassel. You will have these tassels to look at and so you will remember all the commands of the LORD, that you may obey them and not prostitute yourselves by going after the lusts of your own hearts and eyes. Then you will remember to obey all my commands and will be consecrated to your God. I am the LORD your God, who brought you out of Egypt to be your God. I am the LORD your God.' "*

Every time they saw these tassels, they were reminded that God is the One who supplied their needs. In fact, I believe it is no coincidence that God first instructed His people to wear these tassels during their wilderness wanderings, a time when they had to depend on God for their daily needs, as well as trust Him with their future. Therefore, I believe this woman knew exactly where she wanted to touch Jesus, because in the moment of her desperation, she was literally taking hold of the promises of God! In other words, she had Jesus by faith. She had him at his word and at this point, Jesus was not about to let her go. She came to Jesus to be healed, and she received much more from him . . .redemption, life and salvation.

Redemption as a Spiritual Model

Although Nouwen's work entitled, "The Wounded Healer" (1979) is considered a classic book that talks about the role of the pastor as a wounded healer, his words are certainly relevant to anyone who engages in a helping ministry to others:

> *Who can save a child from a burning house without taking the risk of being hurt by the flames? Who can listen a story of loneliness and despair without taking the risk of experiencing similar pains in his/her own heart and even losing their precious peace of mind? In short: Who can take away the suffering without entering it?*

Certainly, as we are exposed to the losses and pain of others, we get in touch with our wounds. Of course, that's the key to redeeming others. We are able to model redemption to others, since we acknowledge that we have been redeemed, both from our sins and from the on-going wounds and scars we sustain as we are engaged in life and death. So often we deceive ourselves when we believe that the experiences we face in life do not have an effect on us. Somehow what we have been taught from early on, and have been reinforced throughout our lives, we believe we can handle it. But every time we hear about another's tragedy, death, timely or otherwise, we come face to face with our own mortality. Yet despite the uncomfortableness, or as Yalom (1980) would say, "death-anxiety", this is not necessarily a bad thing. We need to be reminded that our time on earth is limited; we only have so many heart-beats in life and hopefully this awakens us to realization that we need to cherish every moment, every hug, every kiss and smile that we receive. The fact is that we do run a risk of being hurt and wounded all over again, but we cannot allow this risk to stifle our attempts to heal others. Moreover, people can be healed from their wounds and turn them into a source of strength, not only in terms of how they cope, but also offer them to others so they can incorporate them into their lives and pass along to others.

I was reminded of this aspect of vulnerability when I counseled "Jenny, "a 16 year old high school girl. By all outward appearances, Jenny had it together. She was student council president, cheerleader, straight-A student, and volunteered in her community. However, being a middle-child of divorced parents (with whom she blamed her mother for the divorce), Jenny lived up to her birth order: She was trying to hold everything, including her family, together. Here's how Jenny described a typical day: She would often pick a fight with her mother before leaving for school. By the time she reached the bus stop, Jenny pulled herself together. All day long she played the role of the model student. When she came home for school, she would begin getting dinner ready, throw in a load of clothes to be washed, straighten up the house. . .all in time to pick another fight with mom when she came home at 6:00p.m. Exhausted from the day, Jenny would then begin her homework around 9:00p.m. By the time Jenny came to me she was starting to "unravel." She had all the symptoms of Major Depressive Disorder for an adolescent. After beginning an anti-depressant medication regimen, Jenny's deeper issues started to emerge. One day, the subject turned to love and relationships. Since it appeared to me that she had no time for dating, I asked her, *"What's your definition of love?"* To which she emphatically replied, *"I don't."* *"Don't what?"* I asked. *"I don't love. Because when you love, you're vulnerable, and when you're vulnerable you get hurt."* Wow! I was amazed that she was way too young to have learned a lesson like that! But then again, being wounded knows no age limits. As we explored her life's mantra in more detail, Jenny started to realize that loving another means being open and vulnerable to rejection, hurt, pain, humiliation, etc. Loving others also means she is able to experience joy, peace, safety, acceptance, physical pleasure and emotional support. Simply put, loving others has the potential to be either life giving and transformational or isolating and painful. Nouwen (2006) would say that both joy and sorrow comes from the same cup, the same heart.

When it comes to redeeming our losses, albeit transitional losses or the death of a loved-one, the grief and bereavement literature agree that the more social support we have during a time of loss, the more we are empowered to assimilate our grief into our everyday lives. This became clear to me when I compared grief reactions among cancer, AIDS-related and suicide bereavement (Houck, 2007). In short, when social support (family members, friends, congregations, etc.) is lacking, grief reactions such as a sense of guilt or responsibility, shame, self-destructive behavior and a sense of being stigmatized, are intensified and create great difficulty for people going through the mourning process.

Therefore, I am convinced that we cannot redeem ourselves from painful losses; we need others. *The story of Jesus raising Lazarus from the dead (John 11:1-44, NIV), illustrates this point:*

Now a man named Lazarus was sick. He was from Bethany, the village of Mary and her sister Martha. This Mary, whose brother Lazarus now lay sick, was the same one who poured perfume on the Lord and wiped his feet with her hair. So the sisters sent word to Jesus, "Lord, the one you love is sick." When he heard this, Jesus said, "This sickness will not end in death. No, it is for God's glory so that God's Son may be glorified through it." Jesus loved Martha and her sister and Lazarus. Yet when he heard that Lazarus was sick, he stayed where he was two more days. Then he said to his disciples, "Let us go back to Judea."

"But Rabbi," they said, "a short while ago the Jews tried to stone you, and yet you are going back there?" Jesus answered, "Are there not twelve hours of daylight? A man who walks by day will not stumble, for he sees by this world's light. It is when he walks by night that he stumbles, for he has no light." After he had said this, he went on to tell them, "Our friend Lazarus has fallen asleep; but I am going there to wake him up." His disciples replied, "Lord, if he sleeps, he will get better." Jesus had been speaking of his death, but his disciples thought he meant natural sleep. So then he told them plainly, "Lazarus is dead, and for your sake I am glad I was not there, so that you may believe. But let us go to him." Then Thomas (called Didymus) said to the rest of the disciples, "Let us also go, that we may die with him."

On his arrival, Jesus found that Lazarus had already been in the tomb for four days. Bethany was less than two miles from Jerusalem, and many Jews had come to Martha and Mary to comfort them in the loss of their brother. When Martha heard that Jesus was coming, she went out to meet him, but Mary stayed at home. "Lord," Martha said to Jesus, "if you had been here, my brother would not have died. But I know that even now God will give you whatever you ask." Jesus said to her, "Your brother will rise again." Martha answered, "I know he will rise again in the resurrection at the last day."

Jesus said to her, "I am the resurrection and the life. He who believes in me will live, even though he dies; and whoever lives and believes in me will never die. Do you believe this?" "Yes, Lord," she told him, "I believe that you are the Christ, the Son of God, who was to come into the world."

And after she had said this, she went back and called her sister Mary aside. "The Teacher is here," she said, "and is asking for you." When Mary heard this, she got up quickly and went to him. Now Jesus had not yet entered the village, but was still at the place where Martha had met him. When the Jews who had been with Mary in the house, comforting her, noticed how quickly she got up and went out, they followed her, supposing she was going to the tomb to mourn there. When Mary reached the place where Jesus was and saw him, she fell at his feet and said, "Lord, if you had been here, my brother would not have died." When Jesus saw her weeping, and the Jews who had come along with her also weeping, he was deeply moved in spirit and troubled. "Where have you laid him?" he asked. "Come and see, Lord," they replied. Jesus wept. Then the Jews said, "See how he loved him!" But some of them said, "Could not he who opened the eyes of the blind man have kept this man from dying?"

Jesus, once more deeply moved, came to the tomb. It was a cave with a stone laid across the entrance. "Take away the stone," he said. "But, Lord," said Martha, the sister of the dead man, "by this time there is a bad odor, for he has been there four days." Then Jesus said, "Did I not tell you that if you believed, you would see the glory of God?" So they took away the stone. Then Jesus looked up and said, "Father, I thank you that you have heard me. I knew that you always hear me, but I said this for the benefit of the people standing here, that they may believe that you sent me." When he had said this, Jesus called in a loud voice, "Lazarus, come out!" The dead man came out, his hands and feet wrapped with strips of linen, and a cloth around his face. Jesus said to them, "Take off the grave clothes and let him go."

Did you catch it? From a theological standpoint, Jesus was the one who spoke life into Lazarus, but then turned to the faith community and instructed them to take off the grave clothes and set him free! Many people, like my friend Matthew, who suffered the stigma of AIDS, go through life with their grave clothes on. These "clothes" take the forms of painful memories, woundedness, and disenfranchised grief. Desperately trying to find the balm of healing from others who can hear their stories, as well as recognize the potential for wholeness in them, turn those wounds of brokenness into scars that testify to the on-going grace of God in our lives.

Christian author Walter Wangerin, Jr. (1994) tells the story that illustrates this point:

Even before the dawn one Friday morning I noticed a young man, handsome and strong, walking the alleys of our City. He was pulling an old cart filled with clothes both bright and new, and he was calling in a clear, tenor voice: "Rags!" Ah, the air was foul and the first light filthy to be crossed by such sweet music. "Rags! New rags for old! I take your tired rags! Rags!" "Now, this is a wonder," I thought to myself, for the man stood six-feet-four, and his arms were like tree limbs, hard and muscular, and his eyes flashed intelligence. Could he find no better job than this, to be a ragman in the inner city? I followed him. My curiosity drove me. And I wasn't disappointed.

Soon the Ragman saw a woman sitting on her back porch. She was sobbing into a handkerchief, sighing, and shedding a thousand tears. Her knees and elbows made a sad X. Her shoulders shook. Her heart was breaking. The Ragman stopped his cart. Quietly, he walked to the woman, stepping round tin cans, dead toys, and Pampers. "Give me your rag," he said so gently, "and I'll give you another." He slipped the handkerchief from her eyes. She looked up, and he laid across her palm a linen cloth so clean and new that it shined. She blinked from the gift to the giver. Then, as he began to pull his cart again, the Ragman did a strange thing: he put her stained handkerchief to his own face; and then HE began to weep, to sob as grievously as she had done, his shoulders shaking. Yet she was left without a tear. "This IS a wonder," I breathed to myself, and I followed the sobbing Ragman like a child who cannot turn away from mystery. "Rags! Rags! New rags for old!"

In a little while, when the sky showed grey behind the rooftops and I could see the shredded curtains hanging out black windows, the Ragman came upon a girl whose head was wrapped in a bandage, whose eyes were empty. Blood soaked her bandage. A single line of blood ran down her cheek. Now the tall Ragman looked upon this child with pity, and he drew a lovely yellow bonnet from his cart. "Give me your rag," he said, tracing his own line on her cheek, "and I'll give you mine." The child could only gaze at him while he loosened the bandage, removed it, and tied it to his own head. The bonnet he set on hers. And I gasped at what I saw: for with the bandage went the wound! Against his brow it ran a darker, more substantial blood - his own!

"Rags! Rags! I take old rags!" cried the sobbing, bleeding, strong, intelligent Ragman. The sun hurt both the sky, now, and my eyes; the Ragman seemed more and

*more to hurry. "Are you going to work?" he asked a man
who leaned against a telephone pole. The man shook his
head. The Ragman pressed him: "Do you have a job?"
"Are you crazy?" sneered the other. He pulled away from
the pole, revealing the right sleeve of his jacket - flat,
the cuff stuffed into the pocket. He had no arm. "So,"
said the Ragman. "Give me your jacket, and I'll give
you mine." Such quiet authority in his voice! The one-
armed man took off his jacket. So did the Ragman - and
I trembled at what I saw: for the Ragman's arm stayed in
its sleeve, and when the other put it on he had two good
arms, thick as tree limbs; but the Ragman had only one.
"Go to work," he said.*

*After that he found a drunk, lying unconscious beneath
an army blanket, and old man, hunched, wizened, and
sick. He took that blanket and wrapped it round himself, but for the drunk he left new clothes. And now I
had to run to keep up with the Ragman. Though he was
weeping uncontrollably, and bleeding freely at the forehead, pulling his cart with one arm, stumbling for drunk-
enness, falling again and again, exhausted, old, old, and
sick, yet he went with terrible speed. On spider's legs
he skittered through the alleys of the City, this mile and
the next, until he came to its limits, and then he rushed
beyond. I wept to see the change in this man. I hurt to see*

his sorrow. And yet I needed to see where he was going in such haste, perhaps to know what drove him so.

The little old Ragman - he came to a landfill. He came to the garbage pits. And then I wanted to help him in what he did, but I hung back, hiding. He climbed a hill. With tormented labor he cleared a little space on that hill. Then he sighed. He lay down. He pillowed his head on a handkerchief and a jacket. He covered his bones with an army blanket. And he died. Oh, how I cried to witness that death! I slumped in a junked car and wailed and mourned as one who has no hope - because I had come to love the Ragman. Every other face had faded in the wonder of this man, and I cherished him; but he died. I sobbed myself to sleep. I did not know - how could I know? - that I slept through Friday night and Saturday and its night, too. But then, on Sunday morning, I was awakened by violence. Light - pure, hard, demanding light - slammed against my sour face, and I blinked, and I looked, and I saw the last and the first wonder of all. There was the Ragman, folding the blanket most carefully, a scar on his forehead, but alive! And, besides that, healthy! There was no sign of sorrow nor of age, and all the rags that he had gathered shined for cleanliness.

Well, then I lowered my head and trembling for all that I had seen, I myself walked up to the Ragman. I told him my name with shame, for I was a sorry figure next to him. Then I took off all my clothes in that place, and I said to him with dear yearning in my voice: "Dress me." He dressed me. My Lord, he put new rags on me, and I am a wonder beside him. The Ragman, the Ragman, the Christ!

If there ever was a major biblical theme echoed in Scripture it's the fact that redemption is everyone's responsibility. We cannot redeem ourselves. It takes others. We need others to reach out to us in order to be restored to where we were before our painful experiences. For grief, redemption takes on a different dimension because we are forever changed by our losses. When we experience loss and grief, we are never the same as we once were. Nevertheless, we have a choice: We can become bitter or better through our wounds and scars. When we become bitter, it takes a toll on us physically, emotionally, even spiritually. Unresolved grief can take years off of our lives without us ever realizing it. Moreover, bitterness also causes us to sacrifice a quality of life, a better life for ourselves. We need the support of others who care about us, not trying to explain why we suffer. Remember Job's friends? The best thing they did for Job was to sit with him for sometimes the pain is beyond words. Words cannot adequately express the soul's anguish. However, there came a time when they did speak and believed they had to explain to Job why he was suffering as he did. According to Eliphaz,

Job's condition was a matter of justice. *"Job, you're getting what you deserve."* Bildad's comments focused more on the scapegoat mentality: *"Job, your children must have sinned and you're being punished for them."* Finally, Zophar heaps the last bit of discouragement as he reinforced his belief in God's vengeance: *"Job, you think this is suffering, well you haven't seen anything yet!"*

Still, how do you take off another's grave clothes? Quite simply: layer by layer. I remember a time when I have never felt the sting of grief so much as when my wife and I experienced our third miscarriage. With two previous miscarriages we *took* extra precautions to ensure everything would go smoothly. It was the beginning of her second trimester and everything was ok, so far. This was also the time when I began to emotionally bond with this child. For us men, bonding with our children typically does not occur until we are actually holding our son or daughter in our arms. Before that, we are kind of spectators to the whole thing. Oh we see the physical changes in our wives: the morning sickness, the irritability, the enlarged belly, cravings for spaghetti, garlic bread, French fries and a chocolate shake at midnight, etc. Expectant mothers on the other hand, bond immediately because of the physical and emotional changes that are taking place in them each day. They are quite in tune with every heart beat and progress. However for me, I started to bond after five months. I remember sitting in theology class, supposed to be taking notes, yet all the while, jotting down first and middle baby names that had a nice ring to them. Then one morning, my wife had noticed she was spotting blood. This was not a good sign and was typically an issue of a problem experienced twice before. However, so as not to alarm me, she did not let me know this was occurring. She left for worked that morning as a RN in a hospital and I went on to class. She said later that instead of reporting to her floor, she immediately went to emergency room and remained there till noon. What started as a simple spotting of blood continued into a full-blown miscarriage. I still remember the look of shock and heartbreak on her face when she came home and explained to me what happened. We both felt like someone had played a cruel joke on us: One minute was are standing firm, the next minute the rug was pulled out from us and we were left face down on the floor, shocked, bewildered, dismayed. Perhaps what added to our emotional and spiritual pain was that we believed (or at least assumed) God wanted us to have children. What reinforced this belief was the fact that the desire to have children intensified year after year. We even went so far to pray for children, believing each time God answered our prayers.

When we picked ourselves up off the floor, metaphorically speaking, I noticed that my wife grieved immediately. However, my grief was delayed. I was in shock. Moreover, when the shock started to wear of, I could feel the rage building up in me, not towards my wife, but towards God for allowing such a cruel joke to be played on us. In the days and weeks that followed, we struggled with breaking the news of the miscarriage to everyone who asked how things are coming along with our plans for the baby. Perhaps the most difficult aspect through it all was not in telling and retelling the story, but having to endure all of the well-intended, yet inappropriate comments from family, friends and fellow grocery store shoppers. They would say things such as: *"Oh, I'm sorry to hear that, but at least you and your wife are young and you can always try again." "It's not that bad, after all you really didn't get to know it, did you?"* And the one statement that ripped my heart to ribbons: *"I guess God doesn't think you're ready for children yet."* Grrrr. Over time I would purposefully avoid people, just so I wouldn't have to endure one more pat answer that did nothing to comfort, but only threw more of the salty brine into an already raw wound. As the months passed, I thought that we would never have children. I found myself envying other fathers playing with their children in the park, sharing a Happy Meal at McDonald's®, or just holding them. My disillusionment with God continued. In those months I spent some of the most intense and raging conversations with God that I have ever prayed. Everybody I talked to just didn't understand what I was feeling. Or, so I thought.

Months later, we received a letter from my wife's grand-mother. The opening sentence of the letter read: *"It's 3:00 in the morning and I believe the Lord woke me up with the two of you on my mind."* Isn't it funny how 3:00a.m. always seems to be the time when God wants to talk to us! Anyway, the five-page letter went on to read how she had been praying for us and how she understood our pain and confusion during this time. She explained how she had lost five children through various means: miscarriages, stillbirths and one accidental death. She also wrote how in spite of our pain, God loves us with an everlasting love and how His grace is there for us each day. Those words hit me right where I was. It's as if her words reached in a scooped out the ache that weighed my heart down like a 100 pound stone. I remember sitting back in the chair after finishing the letter and said to myself: *"Finally, somebody understands!"* No pat answers. No explanations. Just empathy, tenderness and love. This letter was the empathic relief I so desperately craved.

In his book *Lament For a Son* (1992), Christian philosopher Nicholas Woldersdorf, whose son died during a mountain-climbing accident, states: *"If you think your task as comforter is to tell me that really, all things considered, it's not so bad, you do not sit with me in my grief but place yourself off in the distance away from me. Over there, you are of no help. What I need to hear from you is that you recognize how painful it is. I need to hear from you that you are with me in my desperation. To comfort me, you have to come close. Come sit beside me on my mourning bench."*

In the months that followed receiving my wife's grandmother's letter, I felt my rage toward God dissipate. That was until my wife greets me one morning with a pregnancy strip in her hand and a *"Guess what?"* on her lips. Uh oh. I didn't think it would be so soon. Moreover, I still didn't feel ready to trust God again. With each passing day, and the signs that this pregnancy was going full term, I felt more and more disconnected. I just couldn't bring myself to trust God with this again, especially since I was still reeling from picking myself off the floor from the last disillusionment. Finally, the moment of delivery came and I found myself no longer able to hold back my emotions. Holding my son in my arms I felt a wave of peace wash over me as I heard the words, *"Life may not be fair, but God is good"* sink into my soul. It was true. As I held him I look up to heaven and quietly mouthed to God that I was sorry for taking out my disappointment and rage on Him. Somehow, in spite of all the times we blame God for things we simply cannot understand, I believe He understands where that pain comes from.

In the Story of Anne Sullivan: A Life That Makes a Difference, Goodier (2002) states that without Anne Sullivan, there would be no Helen Keller. In fact, if it hadn't been for a compassionate nurse, there would be no Anne.

When Anne was young, she was no stranger to hardship. Due to a childhood fever, she was almost sightless herself. Later on, she was diagnosed as hopelessly "insane" by her caregivers. As a form of punishment, Anne was locked in the basement of a mental institution outside of Boston. On several occasions, Anne would violently attack anyone who came near her, but most of the time she generally ignored everyone in her presence. However, one nurse saw more than just an insane child and made it her mission to show her love and kindness. Every day she visited with Anne as she ate her lunch with her. This nurse also left cookies for her and spoke words of love and encouragement. Soon Anne started to respond to these acts of compassion. Eventually, doctors noticed a change in Anne. Where they once witnessed anger and hostility, they now noted an emerging gentleness and love. They moved her upstairs where she continued to improve and eventually, the day finally came when Anne, the then seemingly "hopeless" child, was released. Anne Sullivan grew into a young woman with a desire to help others as she, herself, was helped by the loving nurse. It was she who saw the great potential in Helen Keller. She loved her, disciplined her, played with her, pushed her, and worked with her until the flickering candle that was her life became a beacon of light to the world.

Although Anne Sullivan indeed worked miracles in Helen's life, it was a loving nurse who first saw the potential in Anne, who forever transformed through tangible redemption. We often think about redemption in terms of the past. But I wonder if we consider looking at the future potential of redemption to work in people's lives, just how much greater aspects of healing people can find from their bereavement.

As previously mentioned, disenfranchised grief poses significant problems for people when faced with the death of a loved-one, but are not afforded the right, role, or capacity to openly grieve as other members of society. For communities of faith, mental health, or health-care providers, being made aware that such stigma still exists within society, is key to helping people work through their grief. In fact, this understanding can be assimilated into a person's preferred bereavement paradigm, e.g., *stages* (Kübler-Ross, 1969), *phases* (Parkes, 1972), or *tasks* (Worden, 2008). People who grieve the loss of a loved-one are often neglected and forgotten. Yet they have specific bereavement needs. One need in particular is to become "enfranchised" by the therapist (Corr, 1998). Giving people permission to grieve openly legitimizes their status as mourners. In fact, therapists need to communicate to the surviving loved-one that society's perception of the death may not necessarily reflect their own experience (Rando, 1993).

Quite often bereaved loved-ones are forced to withhold their feelings from family members and friends, etc., and cover up the nature of the death in order to avoid further judgment and emotional isolation. I remember during the early years of HIV/AIDS the popular phrase "Silence=Death" was used to protest society's denial of the epidemic nature of a disease that was immediately stigmatized (Burkett, 1995). In some instances, grieving the loss of a loved-one to suicide may be particularly troubling to reveal in social settings, especially if a family member is in a position of public authority (Rubel, 2003). However, these simple steps are crucial toward healing one's loss and grief:

- Providing a safe environment where thoughts, emotions, and feelings can be shared
- Active listening to what is being said, as well as what is not said
- Normalizing feelings of loss, grief and mourning
- Expressing empathy toward the person's emotions and situation
- Educating people on the process of mourning

Still, many people may be apprehensive about sharing their stories and feelings because they may have never been given permission to talk about the death before. Although others may assume this kind of permission-giving will be attractive to many, grievers may be skeptical about "good intentions." Too familiar with "guilt by association" judgments rendered by society, people may have difficulty accessing another's empathy. Therefore, grievers (disenfranchised or otherwise) need to be reassured that they not only are viewed by helping professionals as person's of value and worth, but they need to know their loved-one's memory will be afforded the same courtesy.

Tools of tangible redemption

Rando (1993) states that in working with bereaved populations, different types of support may be needed not only to facilitate grief, but also may be required at different times. Such resources include:

- Identify the type of support the mourner requires and what support is desired, e.g., individual verses support group.
- Work with the mourner to identify unmet needs as secondary losses, e.g., loss of income, role, etc.
- Deal with the mourner's feelings about not getting needs for support and why those needs are not getting met.
- Review the mourner's expectations for support to determine whether they are appropriate, and help them readjust them if inappropriate, e.g., self medicating through drugs or alcohol.
- Assess the lack of support to determine whether it is due to a lack of assertiveness or other psychological issues.
- Educate the mourner that support for disenfranchised grief often can be found in support groups and/or printed material. Refer them to these sources.
- Educate the mourner on unrealistic expectations or incorrect information about the mourner's needs.

Pargament et al. (1998) notes that a grieving person's religion and spirituality are also important to address in the mourning process. Whether it is existential issues related to God or the Divine, relationships with others, or finding peace within themselves, many people use some form of religious/ spiritual coping in bereavement. In particular, disenfranchised grievers may find themselves not only being shunned by society but also from their faith communities. Yet despite this kind of harsh treatment, those grieving such deaths (e.g., AIDS-related, suicide, etc.) may not be willing to abandon their religious/spiritual beliefs and practices. Instead, they are finding ways to heal and grow in spite of their losses (e.g., seeking new directions of religious/spiritual growth in their relationship with God and others, embracing familiar faith traditions, creating new rituals of remembrance, memorials and observances, and adapting their lives where the deceased is no longer a part of).

As in any bereavement setting, listening to a survivor's story, especially a person's religious/spiritual story, is a critical part of the process of mourning. Pargament (1997) notes that each person's story must be placed within a greater context of the social and personal context. This provides a framework for assessing two important questions regarding religious/spiritual coping: One, is a grieving person's religion/spirituality leading them in a good direction; and two, is the grieving person taking a good road to get there?

Pargament (1997) states that religion/spirituality can function in the following ways:

- *Preservation*: To use religion/spirituality not necessarily to change but to survive, or to provide stability in everyday life.
- *Reconstruction*: To use religion/spirituality to rebuild prior beliefs about God and the world that may have been challenged by the death of a loved-one.
- *Re-Valuation*: Using religion/spirituality to help people discover new sources of significance, e.g., letting go of old attachments to the loved-one and discovering new ways to invest themselves in other people or endeavors.
- *Re-Creation*: Using religion/spirituality as a means of transforming a person's core significance and his/her approach to life, e.g. giving up of avoidant strategies in search for a closeness with God and others.

By focusing on a person's specific religious/spiritual coping methods, people who desire to be extensions of tangible redemption may be able to identify the different ways religion/spirituality enhances or hinders the mourning process. In fact, this awareness will make it possible to integrate religion/spirituality more fully and effectively into everyday life.

The things that drove us crazy. . .

After officiating at over 100+ funerals, and attending about half that many related to deaths in the family and among friends and colleagues, there's one thing I look forward to, the funeral luncheon. Now don't get me wrong, I am just as honored to officiate at a funeral or memorial service and help loved-ones and friends say goodbye and regain some closure. But the fact is that I love to attend the luncheons that follow. Be it extravagant displays of feasting at banquet halls, to a buffet-style lunch in the basement of a church, even sitting down around a kitchen table, I attend funeral luncheons because that's when you hear the stories. Honestly, at times I have never heard so much laughter and good-natured sharing of stories than when I attend a luncheon following a funeral. And yet these are more than just stories. Yes they are memories, but if you listen closely you begin to hear a peculiar thread woven throughout each stories, namely the things that our loved-ones did to drive us crazy, infuriate us, even have done to get on our last nerve at times, are the things we will miss the most about them.

For example, Mildred was 82 years old when Clarence, her husband of 56 years marriage, died at home. The funeral arrangements were made at the local church and the service was lovely. But afterwards in the church basement, little by little, one story after another was shared about how Clarence was a real prankster. That afternoon, I wore myself out going around to all the tables, trying not to miss the latest story about how Clarence would short-sheet the beds at local motels where newlyweds would be staying. But the stories I cherished came from Mildred herself. She would tell me how Clarence would always eat too much at those all-you-can-eat buffet lines. Then, he spend half night awake with an upset stomach, which of course, kept her awake as she fetched one home remedy treatment after another till he was able to fall asleep. With tears in her eyes she whispered to me, "*I won't know what it is like to sleep a whole night through. I worry that nobody will be able to look after him.*" Fighting back a lump in my throat I replied, "*Well, I think there's someone in heaven who knows how to take care of diarrhea!*" She laughed and hugged me, and told me to get another piece of cake before she'd "bop me on the head." That made my day. Hers too, I suppose.

In the movie, *Good Will Hunting*, Robin Williams explains to Matt Damon that everyone has those little idiosyncrasies that at first glance drive us crazy, but in reality, those features contain the "good stuff." For example, Williams' wife used to expel gas in the middle of the night, wake herself up, but blame him for the unpleasant odor. Embarrassed for her, he went along with it and chalked it all up to the intimacy and weirdness they shared. Strange, but as he put it, he felt honored to see, hear, and yes, even smell that side of her. Nobody else would be privileged to that. And just when you thought it couldn't get any weirder, William's explains, "*You know, it's been two years since Nancy died, and that's the stuff I remember!"* But he wasn't bitter, because he realized those memories were some of the things nobody else saw. Instead, he cherished those things because they were the things that made her his wife.

I am convinced that the things our loved-ones did or said that irritated us, drove us crazy and even at times, got on our last nerve, are the things we will miss the most when they are gone. But, just like in *Good Will Hunting*, these are the memories we will relish because they are gems. They are what made our spouses, our spouses. They are what made our mothers and fathers, our mothers and fathers. Grandparents, siblings, co-workers, friends; all have left their impression on us. After my mother died, my sisters and I sat around the kitchen table with a big box of old photos. With every snap shot it seemed as though a new story would be created, perhaps told from different perspectives, but nonetheless, told from a grief that needed a context to make sense of our world and honor the lives of those whom we called family.

Since that day when I first held my son in my arms, I have kept a jar of broken glass on my desk. Every now and again I pick it up just to hold, look and listen to it. Holding this jar always reminds me of two things: Our brokenness and God's wholeness. When I look at it closely, I notice the sharp-edged fragments of a once whole vase. I listen carefully to the shards as they clang when I shake the jar. I also am reminded of the disillusionment of people as they ask: *"Will I ever be made whole again? There are so many frag-*

mented pieces. *I am shattered spiritually, mentally and phys-ically as I stand before God, bearing the scars of my wounds. How will I ever be put back together?"*

One of the most powerful realizations of healing our brokenness came to me when I was celebrating Holy Communion one Sunday. As was typical of Communion Sundays, I would hold up a loaf of bread and tear it in two saying, *"And Jesus took the bread, and after he had given thanks and blessed it, he broke it, gave it to his disciples and said, 'Take and eat this all of you. For this is my body broken for you.' And likewise holding up the Cup Jesus said, 'This cup contains my blood, the blood of the new and everlasting covenant, poured out for you and for many for the forgive-ness of sins. As often as you eat this bread and drink this cup, do this is remembrance of me."* One Sunday, the meaning of the fragmented pieces of glass and the significance of the breaking of the bread came together. I began with my usual blessing of the communion elements, but when I came to the breaking of the bread, I paused. As I tore the loaf in two, signifying the brokenness of Jesus' body, I rejoined the two halves together and said, *"Indeed this is Christ's body that has been broken for us; broken, so that in our times of suf-fering brokenness, broken promises, shattered dreams, and broken spirits, we can be made whole."* What a powerful realization of the grace of God in one of the most sacred moments in worship!

Author John O'Donahue (2004) tells a similar story of how work done with the heart creates beauty, even in the midst of brokenness.

The emperor of Japan possessed a very old and very costly vase. It was an unique masterpiece in the art of chinaware. One day, somebody knocked it down by accident, and it broke into a thousand pieces. The fragments were carefully collected, and the most skillful master-potter of the whole empire was commissioned to put the vase together again. He tried very hard, but he failed, and had to pay for it with his head. The emperor put the difficult task to the second-best potter in the empire, but alas he failed as well. This repeated itself for many weeks, until all namely master-potters of the realm were beheaded, since none of them had succeeded in putting the exquisite vase together again.

In the end only a single artist was left, an old Zen-monk living with his young pupil in a cave in the mountains. On the emperor's call he came to the palace, took the broken pieces with him and carried them to his humble workshop. Then he set to work. After several weeks the monks showed the results of his endeavor to his pupil. The vase had resurrected in its flawless beauty. The two monks wandered back to the city and delivered the vase to the palace. The emperor was overly happy, and the whole retinue praised the perfection of the restored masterpiece. The old monk was richly rewarded and gracefully dismissed.

One day, the young pupil was just rummaging around for something in the workshop, when he unexpectedly discovered the broken scraps of the old vase. He ran to his master and exclaimed: "Look at these pieces, not at all did you put them back together again! However did you only manage to create a vase that is as beautiful as the shattered one?!" The old monk replied: "If you put yourself to work with a heart full of love you will always be able to create something beautiful."

Many times we look at our brokenness, shattered pieces from our wounds, and wonder how they can be put back together. In those moments, Jesus tells us to "Come." Many times we ask ourselves, *"Will I ever be made whole again?"* In those moments, Jesus tells us to "Come." Jesus tells us to come as we are, broken pieces and all, and piece by piece, our lives can be reassembled, not in the way that is familiar to us, but into a vessel that is, ironically, stronger in the cracks. Indeed, if we place ourselves into the hands of Christ, who puts himself to work with a heart full of love toward us, we will discover that he is able to create something beautiful out of the rubble.

Bibliography

Ainsworth, M. D. S., Blehar, M. C., Waters, E., & Wall, S. (1978). *Patterns of attachment: A psychological study of the strange situation*. Hillsdale, N.J.: Erlbaum.

Archer, J. (1999). *The nature of grief: The evolution and psychology of reactions to loss*. New York: Routledge.

Black, K. (1996). *A healing homiletic: Preaching and disability*. Nashville: Abingdon Press.

Bowlby, J. (1958) *The Nature of The Child's Tie to His Mother,* International Journal of Psychoanalysis, *39,* 350-73.

Bowlby, J. (1969) <u>*Attachment, Vol. 1 of attachment and loss*</u>. New York: Basic Books.

Bowlby, J. (1980). *Attachment and loss, volume 3: Loss.* New York: Basic Books, Inc.

Burkett, E. (1995). *The gravest show on earth: America in the age of AIDS.* Boston: Houghton Mifflin.

Catalan, J. (1995). *Psychiatric problems associated with grief.* In L. Sherr (Ed.), *Grief and AIDS.* Chichester, UK: Wiley Press.

Connell, J. P., & Goldsmith, H. H. (1982). A structural modeling approach to the study of attachment and strange situation behaviors. In R. N. Emde & R. J. Harmon (Eds.), *The development of attachment and affiliative systems* (pp. 213-243). New York: Plenum.

Corr, C. (1998). *Enhancing the concept of disenfranchised grief. Omega, 38,* 1-20.

Corr, C.; Nabe, C.; & Corr, D. (2003). *Death and dying, life and living, fourth edition.* Belmont, CA: Wadsworth/ Thompson Learning, Inc.

Doka, K. & Morgan, J. (1993) *Death and spirituality (death, value and meaning).* Amityville, NY: Baywood Publishing Company.

Doka, K. (Ed.). (2002). *Disenfranchised grief: New directions, challenges, and strategies for practice.* Champaign, IL: Research Press.

Estadt, Barry K. (1991). *Profile of a Pastoral Counselor.* In Pastoral Counseling, second edition. Englewood Cliffs, NJ: Prentice-Hall, Inc.

Freedman, D. (ed.) (1992). *The anchor bible dictionary, volume six.* New York: Doubleday Publishers.

Freud, S. (1917). Mourning and melancholia. Reprinted in: J. Strachey (trans. and ed.), *Standard edition of complete psychological works of Sigmund Freud,* Volume 14. London: Hogarth Press and Institute of Psychoanalysis (1957).

Goodier, S. (2002). A Life that makes a difference. Life Support System Publishing.

Goffman, E. (1986). *Stigma: Notes on the management of the spoiled identity.* NY: Touchstone.

Harlow, H. (1959). Love in Infant Monkeys. *Scientific American* 200 (June 1959):68, 70, 72-73, 74.

Hesse, H. (2005) *Siddhartha.* Boston: Shambhala Publications, Inc.

Holmes & Rahe (1967). Holmes-Rahe life changes scale. *Journal of Psychosomatic Research,* Vol. 11, pp. 213-218.

Houck, J. (2007). A comparison in grief reactions in cancer, HIV/AIDS and suicide bereavement. *Journal of HIV/ AIDS and Social Services, 6(3).*

Lindemann, E. (1944). Symptomatology and management of acute grief. *American Journal of Psychiatry, 101,* 141-148.

Lindemann, E. (1986). *Beyond grief: Studies in crisis intervention.* Northvale, NJ: Jason Aronson, Inc.

Jacobs, S. (1999). *Traumatic grief: Diagnosis, treatment, and prevention.* Philadelphia: Taylor and Francis.

Jeffreys, J. Shep (2005). *Helping grieving people: When tears are not enough. A handbook for care providers.* New York: Brunner-Routledge.

Klass, D.; Silverman, P. & Nickman, S. (1996). *Continuing bonds: New understandings of grief.* Washington, DC: Taylor and Francis.

Kubler-Ross, E. (2007). *On grief and grieving: Finding the meaning of grief through the five stages of loss.* New York: Scribner.

Larsen, E. (1994). *Stage II recovery: Life beyond addiction.* New York: Harper One.

Lazare, A. (1979). Unresolved grief: In A. Lazare (ed) *Outpatient Psychiatry: Diagnosis and Treatment.* Baltimore: Williams and Wilkins, p. 498-512.

Main, M., & Solomon, J. (1990). Procedures for identifying infants as disorganized/disoriented during the Ainsworth Strange Situation. In M. T. Greenberg, D. Cicchetti, & E. M. Cummings (Eds.), *Attachment in the preschool years* (pp. 121-160). Chicago: University of Chicago Press.

Moultman, J. (1993). *The crucified Christ: The cross of Christ as the foundation and criticism of Christian theology.* Minneapolis: Augsburg Fortress Press.

Nader, K (1997). Childhood traumatic loss: The interaction of trauma and grief. In C. Fidgley, B. Bride, and N. Mazza (eds.), *Death and trauma: The traumatology of grieving*. Washington, DC: Taylor and Francis.

Neimeyer, R.; Prigerson, H. & Davies, B. (2002). Mourning and meaning. *The American Behavioral Scientist, 46* (2), pp. 235-254.

Nouwen, H. (1979). *The wounded healer: Ministry in contemporary society*: NY: Image Doubleday.

Nouwen, H. (1992). *The return of the prodigal son: A homecoming*. New York: Doubleday.

Nouwen, H. (2006). *Can you drink from the cup?* Notre Dame, IN: Ave Maria Press

O'Donohue, J. (2004). *Anam Cara: A book of Celtic wisdom*. Harper Perennial.

Pargament, K. I. (1997). *The psychology of religious coping: Theory, research and practice*. New York: The Guildford Press.

Pargament, K. I.; Smith, W.; Koenig, H. G. & Perez, L. (1998). Patterns of positive and negative religious coping with major life stressors. *Journal for the scientific study of religion, 37, 710-725.*

Parkes, C.M. (1972). *Bereavement: Studies of grief in adult life.* New York: International Universities Press, Inc.

Rando, Therese (1993) *Treatment of complicated mourning.* Champaign, IL: Research Press

Rando, T. (2000). *Clinical dimensions of anticipatory mourning: Theory and practice in working with the dying, their loved ones, and their caregivers.* Champaign, IL: Research Press.

Rubel, B. (2003). The grief response experienced by the survivors of suicide. Retrieved November 6, 2002 from www.griefworkcenter.com.

Rupp, Joyce. (2009). *Praying our goodbyes: A spiritual companion through life's loses and sorrows.* Notre Dame, IN: Ave Maria Press.

Sadock, B. & Sadock, V. (2002). *Kaplan and Sadock's synopsis of psychiatry: behavioral sciences/clinical psychiatry.*

Wangerin, Jr., W. (1994). *The ragman and other cries of faith.* San Francisco: Harper.

Worden, William (2008). *Grief counseling and grief therapy: A handbook for the mental health practioner, fourth edition.* New York: Springer Publishing Company.

Yalom, I. (1980). *Existential psychotherapy.* New York: Basic Books.

Yalom, I. (2009). *The gift of therapy: An open letter to a new generation of therapists and their patients.* New York: Harper Perennial.

CPSIA information can be obtained at www.ICGtesting.com
260215BV00001B/255/P